Meth

"With millions of Americans confronting the life-or-death issue of methamphetamine addiction, *Meth: The Home-Cooked Menace* provides an insightful look at the devastating effects of this insidious drug and offers policymakers the critical information needed to address this public health crisis."

— JIM RAMSTAD, U.S. representative

"This riveting chronicle of the modern methamphetamine menace brings home the human suffering of this epidemic, which, unlike the earlier heroin and cocaine epidemics, is concentrated in rural areas and small towns. Reading this book will change the way you think about meth and about drugs."

— ROBERT L. DUPONT, M.D., first director of the National Institute on Drug Abuse, president of the Institute for Behavior and Health, Inc., and author of *The Selfish Brain: Learning from Addiction*

Meth

THE HOME-COOKED MENACE

Dirk Johnson

Hazelden
Center City, Minnesota 55012-0176

1-800-328-0094
1-651-213-4590 (Fax)
www.hazelden.org

©2005 by Hazelden Foundation
All rights reserved. Published 2005
Printed in the United States of America
No portion of this publication may be reproduced in any manner
without the written permission of the publisher

Library of Congress Cataloging-in-Publication Data

Johnson, Dirk.
    Meth : the home-cooked menace / Dirk Johnson.
        p. cm.
    Includes index.
    ISBN-13: 978-1-59285-305-2 (pbk.)
    ISBN-10: 1-59285-305-6 (pbk.)
        1. Methamphetamine abuse. I. Title.

    HV5822.M38J64 2005
    362.29'9—dc22

                                                            2005051358

09 08 07 06 05   6 5 4 3 2 1

Cover design by David Spohn
Interior design by Rachel Holscher
Typesetting by Stanton Publication Services, Inc.

For Henry, Nora, Harlan, and Amanda

CONTENTS

ACKNOWLEDGMENTS

With appreciation and admiration, I thank the people who shared their stories of addiction, recovery, and hope. Without their courage to speak about old ghosts and painful times, this book would not exist.

I thank the editor of this book, Karen Chernyaev, for her wisdom, creativity, and patience. A debt of gratitude is owed to my leaders at *Newsweek* magazine, especially Mark Whitaker, Jon Meacham, Marcus Mabry, Tom Watson, and Lisa Miller. I drew from the inspiration of many trusted colleagues, including Tom McNamee, Jim Ritter, and Jack Higgins.

My parents, Karen Lyons and Glen Johnson, were there for me in every way, as they always have been. My sisters, Cynthia Chereskin, Rachel Strack, and Jennifer Johnson, gave needed encouragement, as did the rest of my clan: Donna Johnson, Jerome Lyons, Ben Chereskin, Ted Strack, and Rich Neubauer. In my research I was aided by Andrew Henson, a deputy sheriff in Whiteside County in Illinois. I was honored with the kindness of Margie and Steve Wilkins and the steadfast friendship of Richard and Theresa Johnson.

My children, Amanda, Harlan, Nora, and Henry Johnson, valiantly put up with a stressed, whiskered father and a house littered with scrawled notes. Their talents are a source of amazement and deep pride, and their love and goodness have been gifts that sustain me in every way.

I am forever thankful for Tara Wilkins, a remarkable and beautiful woman whose intellect and soulfulness have enriched this book, and my life.

Reprint acknowledgments:

The Society for Neuroscience brain scan, © 2005 by the Society for Neuroscience, is reprinted with permission from the *Journal of Neuroscience*, Volkow, Nora, et al., "Loss of Dopamine Transporters in Methamphetamine Abusers Recovers with Protracted Abstinence," 21, no. 23 (December 1, 2001): 9414–18.

The excerpt from Penny's letter to the London police on page 126 is reprinted with permission from Penny Wood.

CHAPTER ONE

The Magic of Meth

Just after midnight on a frigid, snowy January night in Nebraska, police dispatchers took a frantic call. "I feel very threatened," said a young man named Mike, his voice trembling. "My girlfriend and I are lost and freezing." Their black pickup truck had skidded off an icy road, he explained, leaving them marooned in a wooded field.

The dispatchers could hear panic in the young man's voice. Trying to calm him, the police asked for their whereabouts. "The Mandalay apartment complex," he told them. But dispatchers were puzzled. The Mandalay was in Omaha. The cell signal was coming from far outside the city.

"That just doesn't make sense," the dispatcher said. Mike soon became frustrated and hung up. Then his girlfriend called. Over the next few hours, the young couple would call police in four Nebraska counties, insisting again and again that they were at their Omaha apartment at Seventy-fifth and Poppleton streets.

Dispatchers knew that could not possibly be true. They

sensed something was playing tricks with the minds of these young people. One dispatcher, growing worried and impatient, gave it to them straight: "You're going to need to find out what is the closest street, so I can send you some help."

It was a life-and-death race against the clock. Temperatures had plummeted to four degrees below zero. A wicked wind was whipping across the plains. The couple's very survival hinged on them being able to give an accurate description of where they were. Police worked feverishly, quizzing Mike about his surroundings. The young man said they had gotten out of the truck and were searching for shelter. He said they were near a pond or a lake. He saw a gravel pit. He saw a crane. He saw a brick shack. All signs pointed to them being stranded in the countryside. But no fewer than twenty-two times, Mike and his girlfriend vowed that they were at the Mandalay complex.

"That just doesn't make sense, okay," the dispatcher told them. "So let's try to rethink it here, okay?"

Something was deeply wrong with how this young couple saw the world around them. It soon became obvious they were hallucinating.

Mike told the dispatchers he saw some two hundred people walking across a pond. He said he called out to them but that they couldn't speak English. "We've tried, we asked for help," he said. "We begged." He said the shack, which could provide shelter, was surrounded by a pack of vicious, howling dogs.

The young woman, meanwhile, related to dispatchers a bizarre sight. She claimed she saw "a lot of Mexicans and African Americans and they're all dressed up in, like, these cult outfits." She said the people were taking automobiles apart, piece by piece, and moving the car parts up into trees.

Mike took the phone, imploring, "Can you please send somebody here now?"

Officers tried everything to bring the couple to their senses. Patty, a night shift dispatcher, tried her best, using the tone of a distressed mother trying to guide a confused child.

"Mike, Mike, I want to help you so bad, hon," she said. "I want to find out where you're at."

From the cell signal and the description of the gravel pit, a dispatcher speculated the couple was near the Platte River in Sarpy County.

"Are you near Iske," a dispatcher asked, referring to a tiny Nebraska town, "or are you near the river?"

Mike stumbled for an answer. "I'm guessing it's . . . um, probably it's . . ." Then he began to cry. "Oh, I don't know for sure."

The dispatcher tried to encourage him. "You don't want to give up, do you?"

Mike responded, "No, I don't."

"I don't either," the dispatcher answered.

The young man was breathing hard. It sounded as if he was walking fast. "I'm freezing and my girlfriend is freezing, and . . ."

"That's why we want to help you," the dispatcher answered.

"Help then, please!" Mike called out.

"That's why I'm saying, please, please, please, Mike, I need you to think about it, okay?" the dispatcher prodded.

At one point, the dispatchers could hear his anguished cry.

"My cell phone's dying," he said. "You're my last chance here."

The next day, Mike Wamsley's frozen, lifeless body was found near the Platte River. It took searchers another six days to find the body of his friend, Janelle Hornickel. They were both just twenty years old.

They died of hypothermia. But tests on the young couple would discover the real culprit: methamphetamine.

Mike and Janelle had been ingesting a homemade version of this drug, also known as "crank" or "speed," a powerful combination of "cooked" over-the-counter chemicals. The drug makes people feel powerful, almost bulletproof. But after repeated use, it can drive users insane with hallucinations and paranoia and make a mockery of their judgment.

On the frigid night of their deaths, neither Mike nor Janelle were wearing a winter coat. Mike was found in a sweatshirt. Janelle was wearing a hooded T-shirt. Inexplicably, they had left warmer clothes back in the pickup, the truck that Mike had told police dispatchers had overturned and was leaking gas. But when police found the truck, it was sitting upright, mired in the snow, with a half tank of gas.

The truck was twenty-three miles from the Mandalay apartments, the place Mike and Janelle were certain they were.

Getting lost in the wilderness of meth has become a North American epidemic. Just a decade or so ago, methamphetamine was scarcely among the leading drugs of abuse. Now it has become the most frightening drug scourge in more than a generation, according to law enforcement agencies, emergency room officials, and drug treatment experts. Police departments in many regions across the United States and Canada say methamphetamine now represents 70 to 80 percent of their drug cases. The reason: meth is a cheap buzz. Instead of paying a high price for the drug through normal channels, users have learned how to concoct an inexpensive variety of meth with over-the-counter chemicals and cold remedies. It is cooked in countless little "mom and pop" labs, like modern-day booze stills, which have overwhelmed law enforcement efforts to stop them.

Federal surveys indicate that a staggering 12 million Americans have used meth. More than 6 percent of high school seniors have tried meth at least once. Perhaps most shocking, some 4 percent of the nation's eighth graders have used the poisonous drug. In 2004, more than 17,000 meth labs were seized, compared to 7,500 in 1999. In the past decade, the number of meth addicts admitted to treatment centers has grown nearly tenfold. Meth abusers now account for more than 5.5 percent of all people seeking help for alcohol and other drug problems, up from 1 percent in 1992.

Once a West Coast phenomenon, meth today is hitting hard in the heartland. About half of the meth labs confiscated in the last few years were seized in the Midwest. Missouri had more labs confiscated than any other state. But meth is working its way across the country and finding its way into the neighborhoods of big cities. If meth isn't now a problem in some regions, police predict glumly, it soon will be.

If you saw meth on a kitchen counter—often a dirty-looking crystalline powder—you might mistake it for crumbs and just sweep it into the trash.

Or you might kill for it. People on meth do crazy things.

A derivative of amphetamine, meth is a powerful stimulant that can seemingly turn a mere mortal into Superman, and then into a scarecrow.

The drug has dozens of monikers: "crank," "glass," "ice," "boo," "speed," "tick-tick," "jet fuel," "chicken feed," "scootie," "trash." By any name, it is perhaps the most frightening drug sweeping America today. Meth is now the second-most commonly used illicit substance, after marijuana, and it is doing staggering harm to families, degrading rural environments, overwhelming police forces, and sapping county social services of their resources.

Meth shares some characteristics of other stimulants, such as cocaine. Stimulants intensify brain and body functions. But meth, which is man-made, is far more powerful than plant-derived cocaine. Smoking meth produces a high that lasts eight to twelve hours, compared to a cocaine high that lasts twenty to thirty minutes. It takes the body twenty-four hours to rid itself of 50 percent of meth. It takes the body just one hour to rid itself of 50 percent of cocaine. Meth can be eaten, smoked, snorted, or injected.

Making meth is as dangerous as using it. Meth is commonly manufactured in makeshift labs in rural areas—kitchens, trailers, barns, abandoned vehicles—where the stench of its cooking can go undetected. The ingredients to make meth are legal, cheap, and easy to buy at the local drug or hardware store: cold tablets, paint thinner, camping fuel, fertilizer, iodine, drain cleaner, rock salt, battery acid, the striker strips on matchboxes, even kitty litter. The key to making meth is extracting the active chemical from cold remedies, ephedrine or pseudoephedrine, by mixing the tablets in a solvent. The methamphetamine base is created by boiling the ephedrine with iodine, red phosphorous, and water for several hours.

The chemicals used to make meth are flammable or corrosive, and a misstep—such as fastening a lid too tightly during the boiling—can blow a house to Kingdom Come. Cooking of the drug has caused more than two thousand fires and explosions a year, according to federal authorities. Much of the time, these makeshift labs are in places where children are present. Meth explosions have become so common in some regions that burn units are overcrowded. Jeffrey Guy, director of the Vanderbilt Regional Burn Center in Nashville, Tennessee, said that "hardly a night goes by" that someone doesn't come in for emergency treatment from meth burns or inhalation of the toxic chemicals used in making the drug. A majority of these victims are young men without insurance. Treatment for burn injuries can cost

$1 million or more. "The costs are jeopardizing hospitals and burn units," said Guy. "It's creating an enormous financial burden." The cost can be worse than just money. At many of these explosions, children are present. In Riverside County in California, a forty-year-old mother was cooking meth at her kitchen stove when it exploded. Her three children, all preschoolers, died in the blast.

Amphetamine, which is similar to methamphetamine in chemical composition, was first synthesized by a German chemist in the late nineteenth century. Methamphetamine, more powerful and easier to make, was derived by a Japanese chemist in 1919. The drug became widely used during World War II to keep soldiers awake and focused for long periods, such as on bombing missions. When soldiers came home, they often brought meth habits with them. Japan, in particular, experienced an epidemic of people shooting meth into their bodies after the war. In America, meth was legally produced in the 1950s and sold over the counter as Methedrine. It was popular among homemakers, college kids, athletes, truck drivers—anybody who needed the extra oomph to make it through the day or night. Into the 1960s, doctors prescribed speed for housewives who wanted to lose weight and get plenty of housework done in a hurry. Still today, meth is legally produced. It is sold in the United States under the trade name Desoxyn. In rare circumstances, it is prescribed for the treatment of obesity, attention deficit disorders, and narcolepsy.

During the 1970s, meth use was associated with outlaw motorcycle gangs in California. The drug was given the nickname "crank" because it was smuggled in the crankcases of motorcycles. The biker gangs used the drug and made money on it. It was a lucrative market, and during the 1980s, biker gangs were shoved aside by highly organized Mexican syndicates. They built superlabs that produced thousands of pounds of meth, often in tablet form, which was smuggled across the border and sold to American distributors. "These guys were not addicts, but sophisticated businessmen," said Rusty Payne, a spokesman for the Federal Drug Enforcement Administration. "They're not your typical gangs who drive hot rods and beat people up. They're savvy, and they're equipped with a lot of technology." The Mexican cartels are still in business, producing perhaps half of all the meth found in the United States. While they usually manufacture south of the border, they sometimes set up shop in Arizona or California. In a single bust in California in 2001, law enforcement agents seized nearly 700 kilograms of meth—enough to supply thousands of people with the drug. In its finished product, meth can be very expensive. A gram can sell for up to $125. An ounce can cost users $1,700. A pound of meth can bring $13,000.

In the mid-1990s, American users of the drug discovered they could make a less pure form of meth themselves, some by copying recipes found on the Internet. By buying common household chemicals, these "mom and pop" operators could make an ounce of meth for as little as $70 or $80. That could amount to a tidy profit when dealing the drug. More often, the meth makers simply made it for their own use and for friends and family. One clan lab can produce enough meth to supply the cook and six other users. The cheap, easy method of making the drug began a virtual prairie fire of meth production. Missouri and Iowa are now among the leaders in meth production.

The lure of meth can seem magical. At first, the drug produces stunning bursts of energy, a feeling of euphoria, heightened powers of concentration, a buoyant sense of self-esteem, and an enhanced sex drive. It seduces people working long hours at grueling jobs, like factory workers and truck drivers;

young parents, who must wake late in the night to tend children and then rise early for demanding jobs; overweight girls and young women struggling to fit society's ideal of body image; people who simply want a temporary escape or who are searching for a way to feel better about themselves and the world around them.

Like all drugs, meth changes the chemistry of the brain. It promotes the release of large amounts of the feel-good neurotransmitters dopamine and serotonin in the limbic system, the part of the brain that governs instinctual feelings like hunger and sex drive. In short, it makes people feel great. This is the "rush" or "high" that meth can deliver. It's as if users are being bathed by a bright, warm light. "It was like, 'Wow!—this is amazing,'" said Thomas, a thirty-three-year-old Illinois man who is now in recovery. "I felt smarter, stronger, better looking, more articulate. I felt like I was simply a much better person. For the first time, I felt like the person I was meant to be."

The sense of euphoria from meth mimics the signals the brain produces when it rewards people for doing the kinds of things needed for human survival. It's the limbic system that provides the pleasurable feeling that comes with eating a nutritious meal or having sex. As meth produces the abundance of dopamine, the sex drive goes into high gear. Men find they can have sex for long periods, over and over—at least in the beginning. Frequently, sex becomes an obsession. Pornography is almost always found at meth labs. In some cases, circles of meth users have orgies or trade sex partners, sometimes videotaping their encounters. In the gay community, meth's power to enhance the libido has led to sexual free-for-all orgies on "the circuit," as the drug parties are known. On meth, everything is about feeling good.

Over time, this flood of mood-enhancing neurotransmitters

triggered by meth starts to interfere with rational decision making, which is controlled by the prefrontal cortex. That part of the brain holds the intellectual powers that remind people to take care of business: to go to work or to study for a test or to dress the children, rather than play video games and munch on candy all day. Meth obscures people's ability to realize what needs to be done in their lives.

The power of drugs like meth to change brain behavior has been demonstrated in studies of mice. Millions of years of evolution have taught rodents to seek quiet, dark places in order to avoid predation. But when researchers feed drugs to mice for a time, the critters will run into lighted places, searching for the high-inducing substance. In essence, the mice are risking their lives in order to get to the drug. People addicted to meth do the same thing. They stop going to work. They stop paying bills. They neglect their children. Nothing in the world matters but meth.

Research has shown that even the thought of meth can trigger the dopamine-releasing mechanism in the brain. In that way, the meth user is similar to the dogs in Pavlov's famous experiment, where the animals were taught to associate the ringing of a bell with food and then drooled at the mere sound of the bell, even when there was no food available. Meth addicts talk of experiencing an exciting "mini-high" when they secure the drug, even before they use it.

For a while using seems to work, but over time, the high that meth once provided becomes a mockery, and regular meth users eventually pay a hideous price. They develop sores all over their bodies from scratching at what seems like a thousand bugs gnawing at them. Their gums become diseased. Their teeth rot and fall out. They become emaciated and hollow-eyed. On meth, a person of thirty can pass for a person of fifty or more. The police call meth users "tweakers" because they tend to jerk and twitch like people suffering from Parkinson's disease, a severe nervous disorder.

Meth can cause blood pressure to soar so high a user can suffer a stroke. It can damage neurons in the brain, causing foggy thinking and severe memory loss. Meth use with dirty needles can spread hepatitis and HIV. Meth can cause respiratory problems, irregular heartbeat, and extreme anorexia. Convulsions from meth can be deadly.

After using meth long enough, people start to go crazy, as the drug profoundly affects the central nervous system, often causing brain damage that some researchers fear may be irreparable. Psychiatrists say longtime meth users display symptoms that are virtually indistinguishable from those of a paranoid schizophrenic. Sleepless for days or weeks, they start seeing danger in every shadow, sensing a threat from every sound. They act in obsessive ways, taking things apart and putting them back together, over and over.

The psychology of meth users becomes jumbled. Their memory becomes impaired. They have problems solving simple math equations, such as making change at the store or reading a car's gasoline gauge. Instead of feeling a euphoric high, meth users become skittish and paranoid. They jump at shadows they see in corners or shudder when they hear noises. They stock up on guns. They withdraw from social circles. Family members and friends come to be seen as enemies, plotting the demise of the meth user. Kaitlyn, a twenty-five-year-old Wisconsin woman who used meth daily for two years, said every car seemed to be trailing her, every pedestrian seemed to be spying on her. When she turned on the radio, she believed that the announcers were speaking directly to her. "I was literally going crazy," she said. "It got to the point that I didn't know whether what I was seeing was real or not." It was a logical fear. The hallucinations caused by meth appear to be far more bizarre and intense than the visions conjured by LSD. Part of the problem is sleeplessness. Staying awake for long periods, even without the drug, can cause people to see visions and hear voices. Meth addicts start seeing people who aren't there and, like Mike and Janelle, completely lose track of their bearings.

Meth users ultimately become so paranoid that they have been known to climb into trees on their properties, armed with shotguns, and scan for the thieves or the cops they're sure are coming to get them. When police do arrive, the scene can be fraught with danger. A drug-crazed paranoiac with a loaded gun is a police officer's worst nightmare. The craziness caused by meth can lead to brutal and shocking tragedy. A man, ripped senseless by meth, was driving his van down a highway in New Mexico one afternoon when he decided to toss a "demon" out the window. He thought it would be the end of his problem if he could simply dispose of the evil spirit. But it was no demon he tossed from his vehicle. It was the severed head of his fourteen-year-old son.

People high on meth can become violent. Meth users can become so enraged or psychotic while on the drug that they beat spouses, friends, and children—or sexually abuse them. In rural Idaho, a man high on meth took an iron bar and crushed the skull of his girlfriend's son, a toddler.

To counter the feelings of being wired, and perhaps to get some sleep, users often turn to sedatives or alcohol. Their homes, meanwhile, fall into shambles. Floor carpets get filthy, beds go unmade, dishes are left unwashed. Garbage piles up everywhere. There is often an infestation of mice, rats, cockroaches, and fleas. Scared to death that someone is coming after them, meth users often keep big dogs around to warn of visitors. But they often don't clean up after the canines, and so the mess and stench grows even worse.

As with other addictive substances, the craving for meth can become so powerful that its users give up on everything else—leaving their spouses, quitting their jobs, even abandoning their children. Meth addicts can become swallowed by shame and guilt, loathing themselves for what they've become, for the sordid things they've done while they were "cracked" on the drug, and for the people they've harmed or abused or simply disappointed. They come to believe that no one cares about them, nor should. They lack a spiritual life, thinking themselves too damaged and dirty to possibly be loved or forgiven.

"Many of these were decent, rational, good-hearted people," said Richard Rawson, a drug researcher at the University of California in Los Angeles. "They didn't intend to become addicts. They are people who have made a mistake in judgment. And they've gotten into serious trouble."

Addiction to stimulants happens rapidly, and withdrawal can be hellish. During use, the brain learns to stop producing dopamine and serotonin on its own. It doesn't need to produce them, since the drug is doing all the work. With the brain no longer making dopamine—and meth no longer triggering the production of the feel-good brain chemical—the former user can sink into a deep depression. It's not uncommon for users coming off meth to sleep for three days straight. But when they wake, they likely obsess about using meth again. Life without the drug seems pointless. So they go back to it, often with reckless abandon, and their lives career even more out of control.

To support the habit, it's common for meth addicts to steal or deal. Some meth users become so desperate they end up on the streets, selling their bodies for one more fix. It's not certain how many lives meth has ruined. But experts say one thing is clear: It seems to be growing worse each day.

Mike and Janelle had barely made it out of their teens. They had been pals since the seventh grade in the little Nebraska town of Ord. With a population of just 2,400, deep in the Corn Belt, Ord is the kind of prairie town where people work hard during the week, go to church on Sunday, and do their best to pass along solid values to their children.

People who knew him best say Mike was a good-hearted kid, someone known for his loyalty, good humor, and sense of compassion. But drugs can turn the world upside down. Trouble came early to Mike. He dropped out of school. He never got on track with work. A brother had tried to talk to him about drugs. Mike must have thought he could handle it. No one knows when he started with meth. All that is certain is that when he tangled with this poison, he lost.

Janelle, as far as anyone could tell, seemed to have it all together. She was an honor student, an athlete, and a cheerleader. She belonged to the drama club and sang in the choir. At Creighton University, a Catholic school in Omaha, she was studying business. She belonged to the Delta Zeta chapter on campus. Her sorority sisters had been among those who had joined the search team for her.

Her death left her mother to wonder why. "It's a parent's worst nightmare," Janelle's mom told the *Omaha World-Herald*. "I'm glad I'm as old as I am . . . because I won't have much time before I see her."

The night before they got lost forever, Mike and Janelle had been partying in a house in the small Nebraska town of Kearney, according to police. Authorities cannot be certain if the young couple ingested meth while they were in that home. But when detectives went back to the house to investigate, they found implicating evidence and charged two people at the house with possession of meth. One was Mica Morel, a nineteen-year-old man. The other was his forty-eight-year-old mother, Judith Morel.

Some people on the prairie gasped at the idea of a mother and son being charged with possession of meth. But when it comes to this drug, nothing surprises the police anymore. They've watched it ravage the home front. The sheriff told a local reporter, "If people could come forward and help us with this war, we may be able to win.

"As it is," he added, "we're losing."

CHAPTER TWO

"Mom and Pop" Labs:
Hitting Hard in the Heartland

These guys looked like some bad dudes. One wore a Mohawk. One had bulging biceps and a gaze that said, "Don't look this way." One was tall and skinny and whip-quick, with steely eyes and a Fu Manchu mustache. Another wore a ragged tattoo on his neck with a menacing warning: "PARENTAL ADVISORY."

The leader of the Arkansas group was a tall, beefy man with a Hell's Angels ponytail and shoulders as broad as Texas. His name was Rick. And he meant business.

"Let's go," he fired out, crushing a foam cup as he rose up on slant-heeled cowboy boots. "It's time to rock 'n' roll."

Each of them was packing heat: high-powered handguns called Glocks. But this was no outlaw gang. These were plain-clothes detectives on a hunt for trouble. The cops climbed into two vehicles, a red Trailblazer and a white Suburban, flipped on some music, and headed down the road, looking for meth labs.

For a drug task force, finding meth is like shooting fish in a barrel. The officers knew they would make a bust by the day's end. "They're just everywhere around here," said Rick. "It sometimes seems like everybody and his brother has started a lab." Meth now accounts for about 22 percent of all drug arrests in America. But the numbers are much higher in the middle of the country. In places like Arkansas, police in some counties are making more arrests for meth than for all other drugs combined. And a majority of serious crime has its roots in meth, from theft that helps feed the habit to domestic violence to the sexual abuse that is so often tied the drug. "In rural America, meth is the number one illegal drug—absolutely, positively, end of question," said Rusty Payne, a spokesman for the Federal Drug Enforcement Administration. For people who watch their communities being poisoned by meth, it's difficult to understand why the police aren't putting a stop to it.

"The public is on our butts, saying, 'We want you guys to get rid of this stuff—you aren't doing enough,'" said Rick, shaking his head in frustration. "And they're right to gripe." But it's not that simple.

What makes meth so different from other illegal drugs is the way it can be produced: cheaply and at home. Cracking down on meth is like cracking down on mosquitoes at a summer picnic. No matter how many you catch, they keep coming. Marijuana, heroin, and cocaine are all imported from other countries and are generally distributed by big-time dealers. Police can choke off a major supply with a single major bust. But because meth is manufactured in countless little makeshift labs, a single bust doesn't make a dent. Moreover, covert operations in small towns can be tricky, since everybody knows everybody, including the cops. To make matters worse, police budgets are strapped and jails are overcrowded. Treatment centers, especially in rural areas, are in short supply. For addicts who want to stop using but don't have insurance, the wait for help can last several weeks.

But meth labs pose problems that go far beyond the dangers of the drug: it sickens those who inhale the fumes and it can make a tinderbox of the homes in which the meth is cooked. Federal authorities say about 15 percent of meth labs are discovered because they have blown up or caught on fire. The deadly consequences of these labs has given rise to a bit of gallows poetry: "Meth—it'll kill you if you take it; it'll kill you if you make it."

Dozens of people die in meth lab explosions each year, and hundreds more are severely burned. Most often, it's the meth "cooks" who are most at danger of an explosion, since they hover near the brewing drug. An Arkansas woman was blinded by a fire that flashed into her eyes. She was taken to the emergency room and spent weeks in the hospital. Police say she's out of the hospital now—blind, but still using meth cooked by her "friends." Innocent bystanders can get burned, too. In the little Illinois town of Perry, for example, a meth lab destroyed a mobile home and everything in it—including the lives of two little children. Even people living next door to a meth lab face the risk of fire.

The danger of meth making is made worse by the fact that the cooks and their friends won't call for help in a crisis because they fear being arrested. The loss of precious time in getting an emergency crew to a fire can spell the difference between life and death. In one case, a circle of people were operating a lab in a camper trailer outside a mobile home when the chemicals blew up in the face of the cook, Michael, a man in his mid-thirties. Literally on fire, Michael ran out of the camper, screaming in pain and terror, and rolled around on the ground trying to stop the flames. As Michael lay dying, some in the group set about to destroy the evidence of the meth lab—before calling for emergency help. They were able to get rid of the obvious signs before the police or the ambulance arrived, even though it meant Michael died and another man watched a few burned fingers fall from his hand.

People who accidentally happen upon one of these labs can be in mortal danger, too. Katie Collman, a ten-year-old in a small town in Indiana, headed to the Dollar Store one afternoon to pick up some toilet paper. On her way back, she apparently stopped at the People's Bank for a lollipop, then went to an apartment complex to tell a friend that a dog had been hit by a train. Katie never made it home. Authorities believe she stumbled across a meth lab in one of the apartments. According to an FBI affidavit, one of the meth makers said he and his cohorts "decided to scare her with the hope that she would be intimidated enough to keep her observations to herself." One of the men, according to the FBI, took Katie to a creek in a pickup truck. The little girl's drowned body was found five days later in the creek, her small hands tied tight behind her back. The girl's grieving father, John Neace, seethes every time he passes the run-down apartment buildings. Neace, a factory worker who lives in a trailer, began a campaign in the little town to gather enough donations to buy the buildings, then tear them down.

It doesn't take much education or skill to construct a meth lab. "Any idiot with barely a lick of sense can do it," said one frustrated undercover officer. There are thousands of recipes for meth making on the Internet. A meth lab can be small enough to fit in a suitcase, and even when the equipment and chemicals are in clear view, a meth lab isn't always easy to spot. The average person can walk past a lab without realizing what it is. It doesn't look like a high school chemistry set or mechanical contraption in a scientist's laboratory. It's mostly just a collection of household chemicals and hardware store items—the sorts of things that can be found at home, under the sink or out in the garage. But to law enforcement professionals, there are some telltale signs. The clearest indication is the presence of several empty boxes of cold medicine, like Sudafed. Cops also look for the combination of the chemicals used to make meth—all gathered in close proximity. "You notice when all these chemicals are sitting together, and you notice where they're found," said one cop. "Maybe it's not unusual for a guy to have camper fluid. But why isn't it in the garage? Why is he keeping so much of it in his kitchen?"

The most obvious sign of a meth lab is the smell. The cooking of meth gives off a sharp, stale odor. It's been described as smelling like cat urine or ammonia. The stench is the reason most meth is made in remote places, so that nobody is around to ask questions about the strange odor. Meth makers sometimes wrap the interior of homes and apartments in a plastic sheath to trap the smell of the fumes. But this also makes the toxic fumes more powerful and can make it more difficult to escape an explosion. Doctors in burn units say they see meth cooks and users come in literally peeling melted plastic from their bodies.

People who inhale the fumes of meth being cooked, often including children in the home, can suffer serious health problems. "It blisters and burns your lungs and your nostrils," said Pete Rapstine, an emergency medical technician for a fire department in Arizona. "It can destroy your brain cells." A study by the National Jewish Medical and Research Center in Denver, Colorado, has found that the poisons of meth are far stronger than originally believed and can linger in homes for long periods, causing serious respiratory ailments and other problems. Even small doses of the fumes can cause skin and eye irritation, headaches, nausea, dizziness, and throat burns.

"We were surprised by the large amounts of hydrochloric acid and methamphetamine vaporized during the cook," said Dr. John Martyny, the author of the study. "The chemicals spread throughout the house. The methamphetamine is deposited everywhere, from walls and carpets to microwaves, tabletops, and clothing. Children living in those labs might as well be taking the drug directly." The study focused on the cooking of methamphetamine in a scientific laboratory, a house and a motel room, and at fifteen clandestine meth labs on three separate occasions. Each time, the levels of hydrochloric acid exceeded the federal standards of "Immediately Dangerous to Life and Health." Dr. Martyny said these chemicals pose frightening health risks, "especially for small children who explore their environment by crawling and putting things in their mouths."

Even after the labs are shut down and the homes are cleaned, the residue can cause danger to the next inhabitants. Health officials are now expressing concern that these chemicals could act as carcinogens that might cause cancer over long periods of exposure. Already, some people say their children have gotten sick for mysterious reasons, and only later did the parents discover their homes had been used as labs. In some of these cases, tenants have filed suits against landlords for failure to disclose the meth-making activities.

Once the smell gets into a house or apartment, police officers say it's difficult ever to make it smell fresh again. Many places require landlords to tell new tenants if anybody ever cooked meth in a home, since the residue in drains, on counters, in floor crevices, and in the ventilation system can cause health damage to later occupants of a dwelling. Cleaning up a meth lab can cost $15,000. In 2004, taxpayers spent nearly $50 million disposing of the hazardous waste. But experts say a thorough cleanup is crucial: if a surface has visible contamination or staining, complete removal may be necessary. That might mean new drywall, carpets, or counters. The ventilation system must also be cleaned and a new furnace installed. The plumbing may be contaminated from the waste products poured down the drains or toilets. Any gloves, rags, or clothing that touches the contaminants must be disposed of. When all remnants are finally removed, the home must be closed for days, with the heat turned up to burn off what's left of the chemicals. Then the place needs to be aired out for days, windows and doors open, before being inspected again for contamination. In some cases, it's nearly impossible to make a home safe after meth. So the place is simply demolished. Many counties still have no ordinances or guidelines for cleanups.

Meth is also harmful to the environment. Manufacturing a pound of meth can produce up to seven pounds of hazardous waste. These toxic chemicals are usually dumped in storm drains, rivers, or lakes, or they are simply left to fester in a field. The chlorinated solvents and byproducts pose long-term hazards because they can persist in the soil and groundwater for years. Meth poured into streams pollutes water and can kill fish. The labs are sometimes operated deep in national forests or on other public lands. A law enforcement officer for the National Forest Service told *Sierra Magazine*, "We had one mobile-home lab that had been operating for several years on private land within the boundaries of the Sitgreaves National Forest. We found some large ponderosa pines that were one hundred and fifty years old killed off by the fumes." In another park in Arizona, officials found a huge lab that had killed shaggy bark juniper and piñon pine trees. In one case, federal officials had to remove tons of contaminated soil from public lands at a cost of about $100,000. In ranch country, the meth-making poisons have gotten into streams and killed the cattle who drank from the waters. Autopsies on other farm animals have found high levels of toxicity and liver and kidney damage. But authorities say farmers who find the meth chemicals sometimes simply bury the hazardous materials rather than report them, because they will be liable for cleanup costs.

It has become common in rural areas for law enforcement agencies to put up posters that warn people about the signs of meth labs, especially the presence of chemicals or the odor. The education efforts target groups that frequent the outdoors: campers, hikers, snowmobile operators. They are also training service people who work inside houses, such as cable installers and utility personnel, to be aware of any suspicious activity and to report it to the authorities. Clerks at pharmacies are warned to tell police about customers who seem to be buying excessive amounts of cold remedies or who buy those remedies along with ingredients for making meth. Since many states now limit the amount of cold medicine customers can purchase, groups of meth addicts will often go on road trips to store after store, buying two boxes of pills at each retail outlet. In the meth world, this is known as "smurfing." Farmers are stepping up security, too. Anhydrous ammonia, an ingredient that is used to make a particularly strong form of meth, is a crop fertilizer that can be found in fields or barns throughout the Midwest. Farmers who once let tanks filled with anhydrous ammonia sit unprotected are now locking them away in barns, and they are searching their properties to make sure no meth squatters have invaded.

Another sign of a meth lab is heavy traffic at a house— people coming and going at all hours. Meth users typically evolve into a little cult. They have a shared passion and a united need to keep secrets. Sometimes they are friends. In plenty of cases, they are family members—cousins, nephews, even children. Since meth users often stay up all night, carloads of visitors routinely pull up to homes at three or four o'clock in the morning, an odd time for most people to invite company. Meth cooks are increasingly being tied to identity theft, using other people's checks and credit-card numbers to get money for more drugs. These meth users search mailboxes for bills and comb through trash for account numbers.

It's actually garbage that often gives meth cooks away. Detectives look for excessive amounts of trash: a dozen or more bags of garbage being placed on the curb of a small house, week after week. Sometimes detectives will simply stop and pick up the garbage and take it away for inspection. "Yeah, it's easy—we'll steal their trash and just pick through it," said Rick, noting that courts have upheld this technique, which has been used by undercover officers and tabloid gossip reporters. "Once you've put something to the curb, you're saying anybody is free to come and get it. So that's what we do. When it comes to your trash, there's no right to privacy. It's there for anybody in the public to look through. And you know what: you can tell a lot about somebody by looking through their garbage."

Investigators keep a particularly sharp eye out for the tools used to make meth: glass dishes, jugs and bottles, paper towels, coffee filters, thermometers, funnels, blenders, rubber gloves, pails, gas cans, aluminum foil, propane cylinders, hot plates, measuring cups. Some of the signs are more obvious than others, such as syringes or even notes printed from the Internet with titles like "How to Make Methamphetamine."

It's the paranoia of some meth cooks that gives them away. They're so fearful of being detected they sometimes go to absurd lengths to shield the view of outsiders. They hang blankets or quilts over windows. They nail boards over windows or spray-paint the panes black. They pace the grounds outside a house, sometimes for hours, or climb onto rooftops or into high tree branches to peer across the landscape. Or they'll walk out to a squad car patrolling the neighborhood, wave over the officers, and accuse them of harassment—all the while denying that they're doing anything wrong, often without even being asked.

Not long ago, before the drug became such an epidemic, a police officer might simply have thought a meth user to be a bit of an oddball, or perhaps somebody who needed psychological help. But now that meth has become a regular feature of law enforcement work, cops can usually spot a "tweaker" instantly. They're usually just skin and bones, with open sores from picking at their skin. They fidget and twitch. "It's not too hard to spot a tweaker," said Rick. "They're skinny and pock-marked and their teeth are falling out. If they're high, their eyes are so dilated they look like saucers." They are also frequently very dirty. Meth users might not have showered in weeks. They talk a mile a minute. And they trust no one.

Given the paranoid state of mind of meth users, cops know that making a bust can be risky. The International Association of Undercover Officers recently held a five-day seminar in Florida about fighting meth and being wary of its special risks. "If you can help it, you don't make a high-risk entry at all," said Charlie Fuller, a former officer with the office of Alcohol, Tobacco and Firearms. "If they were cooking crack, it wouldn't be as big a deal. But with meth, you never know how they're going to react. So you try to get them to come outside and talk."

At least 20 percent of people involved in meth busts were armed when police arrived, according to federal surveys. A man in Denver last year led police on a one-hundred-mile-per-hour chase before turning and shooting a veteran officer to death, and then killing himself. In one recent bust of a small lab, California police found an assault rifle, two semiautomatic handguns, and a wireless surveillance system. The labs are also sometimes equipped with booby traps to stop intruders or to burn the incriminating ingredients and equipment for making meth. These traps can explode or cause flash fires.

Fire and police officials who respond to meth labs must take extreme caution. "We treat it just like there was a bomb inside," said Pete Rapstine, the emergency technician from Arizona. "Because of the chemicals involved, it can shoot a blast that blows out walls and windows and sends shrapnel flying for a hundred feet or more." If authorities know a meth lab is in active production, or has started a fire, specially trained units go into homes wearing hermetically sealed "moon suits" and masks with breathing apparatus. In some cases, it's the booby traps that pose severe danger. "We're talking booby traps that are like Vietnam-era stuff, like something out of *Death Wish* with Charles Bronson," said Rapstine. "These meth cooks will use anything they can to keep you away—everything up to dynamite." In some cases, the meth producers have constructed devices like rat traps that, when tripped, set a door or board full of sharp nails slamming down on first responders. "I would rather investigate a homicide than a meth lab," Andrew Tafoya, a sheriff's lieutenant in northeastern Arizona, told *Sierra Magazine*. "These labs are a logistical and environmental nightmare."

Most squads prefer to go into a lab when it's not in production, since gunfire added to the toxic chemicals could mean a blowup that would kill everybody. It can make the criminal case more difficult, since it's not illegal to have a meth lab—as long as it's not producing the drug. "But do you want to make the case, or do you want to get hurt?" asked Fuller, who taught one of the classes on meth enforcement. Officers who enter a lab are told to wear masks and special suits that guard against the poisonous fumes of the meth. Several years ago, cops didn't take such precautions. Now officers are worried about long-term damage, similar to the latent consequences suffered by Vietnam veterans exposed to chemical defoliants. "Meth labs are the Agent Orange of law enforcement work," one police expert warned.

It takes much more effort to track meth activity than other drugs. As one undercover officer put it: "I can bust people for crack and have them in jail and be done in an hour." Investigating a meth lab, on the other hand, can take hours. And the initial cleanup can take much of a day. In most cases, police are required to call hazardous-materials specialists who cart away the chemicals. The toxic ingredients are disposed of in special landfills. Waiting for the haz-mat specialists can take hours, so police are tied up for long periods on a meth arrest.

The biggest number of good tips about meth come from telephone calls. Many regions have established toll-free numbers so people can call and report strange goings-on anonymously. Another good source is the people who have been arrested themselves. An undercover officer in New Mexico said he urges those arrested to "flip" on other users or dealers in exchange for lesser charges or for charges to be dropped altogether. "It's part of the drug culture that people are going to rat on each other," the officer said. "You'd be surprised how the toughest, hardest guys will start talking as soon as you slap the cuffs on them. There is no loyalty in the drug world." Sometimes they pay cash to meth users in exchange for information. A fifty-dollar bill is often enough for a meth addict to turn on his or her accomplices. Some of these informants take up snitching full time, going from lab to lab, smoking or snorting with people who think he or she is a friend. These informants, or "narcs," usually keep using the drug themselves, and the police know it. The continued drug use can be ruinous to the health of the informer. But that's a sacrifice that police officials say cannot be avoided. "You let one fish go so you can catch a bunch more fish," said the New Mexico undercover officer.

Rick and his meth-busting crew headed down a winding road at the edge of Hot Springs, Arkansas, on a hazy Tuesday morning. A telephone call had alerted the drug task force of a meth lab in the hilly woods at the edge of town. Rick and his partners rolled down Magic Mountain Road, then turned toward the ranch-style brick-and-frame home that a caller had pinpointed for them. Rolling into the gravel driveway, the cops surveyed the scene. Parked in front were four cars and a van. One had a bumper sticker with an American flag and a slogan calling for prayer in schools. The windows of the house were covered with an unusual and tragically poignant disguise: crayon drawings by kids. The drawings were mostly about having a Merry Christmas. But the holiday season had passed months ago.

"Yep, this is the place," said Rick. The officers swung open the doors of the vehicles and stepped out. A couple of the detectives walked to each side of the house, casing the scene. Another stood near the road, fifty yards away from the house, clutching a high-powered handgun. He is trained as a sniper, and he was watching for trouble, just in case his partners came under attack.

Rick knocked on the front door, and asked if he could come in to talk. A slender woman in her twenties nodded that it was okay. Moving quickly, two detectives walked into the house to look for signs of the deadly drug. Immediately, they detected the faint, pungent odor of meth. At a kitchen table sat three children eating oatmeal for breakfast. The oldest was five years old. The children looked puzzled.

The place was a mess. The walls were streaked with grime.

Dirty clothes were strewn all over the floors. Tables and chairs were piled high with junk. Lightbulbs had gone dead. The sheets on the beds looked like they hadn't been changed in months. A big-screen TV was turned on, blaring loudly. But nobody was watching.

Out of a back room wandered three men, looking dazed. It was obvious they were strung out on meth. One of the cops shot them a look of disgust.

"What's going on?" asked one of them, feigning surprise.

"Like you don't know," one of the detectives muttered under his breath.

The officers continued sifting through the debris in a bedroom. In just a couple of minutes, they found a foil of tin with the residue of meth. The detectives grabbed the handcuffs and slapped them on a man named Tony. He was a ghostlike figure, rail thin and bedraggled, with greasy hair and a pale, sandpapery face. He was forty-one, but looked like a sickly old man. His arms were covered with sores. He smelled putrid. His head bobbed up and down, as if his neck was no longer strong enough to support it.

He was the boyfriend of the kids' grandmother. The kids and their parents had been staying in his house—it is actually owned by Tony's mother—for the past few months.

As the man was led outside, one of the kids called out to his mom, "Is Grandpa Tony going to jail?"

In a dank corner room of the basement, detectives found the man's stash: cans of Drano, boxes of Sudafed, camping lighter fluid, iodine, the sulfur of ripped matches. Since the contaminated goods could be lethal, police immediately called a private company that handles hazardous materials to come and haul them away.

"This is where they were cooking the stuff," said Rick.

"Smell that smell? You get that in a house and you can never get rid of it. Never."

Despite finding the obvious elements of a meth lab, the detectives were unable to charge Tony with the manufacture of the drug, a crime that can bring serious prison time. "The state says we've got to catch them red-handed," said Rick. "We have to see them actually making the stuff—and that's pretty difficult to do." So Tony was arrested on a lesser charge: possession of drug paraphernalia. He would be booked and locked in the Garland County jail for a time. But the cops figured he would probably make bail and likely go back to his trade. Tony was no stranger to law enforcement officials in Hot Springs. It wasn't the first time he'd been arrested on meth charges.

Before being hauled away, Tony stood outside the house on Magic Mountain Road, staring at the ground.

One of the cops glared at him, seething with anger.

"I'm sick of you," the officer screamed, unable to stomach his rage any longer. "I'm so tired of running into you. Are you proud you're a meth cook? Are you proud of that, Tony?"

The officer reddened in the face, his neck bulging. "How could you do this with kids in the house? Three little kids! Tell me! How?"

He drew near Tony, so close he was almost nose to nose.

"You know this stuff can blow up a house," he yelled. "You know that! With kids inside! And you didn't care, Tony. You didn't care." The muscular cop stared him in the eye. "You realize I could be here on a murder charge, don't you?" he demands. "You could have blown up this house and killed those kids."

Whether Tony understood or not was hard to tell. He looked like he was in another world.

Finally, the cop shook his head and walked away, kicking at the gravel in frustration.

The cop's name is John, and he looks as rugged and fit as a Marine at the top of his training. John doesn't need this job. He doesn't do it for the paycheck. The truth is that he has lots of family money. He could walk away from police work and live a comfortable life. He could do whatever he wants. But he has seen the cancer of meth ruin so many lives, tear away at the fabric of his hometown. He wasn't about to turn his back and walk away.

"I've put friends in jail," he later explained. "I've put ex-girlfriends in jail."

It didn't matter who they were. He was going to stop at nothing, he vowed, to fight this menace.

Through the uproar of the arrest, the young mother, wearing jeans and a sweatshirt, was trying to comfort her kids and keep them out of the fray. She explained that she and her husband had been staying in this troubled house because there was no other choice. Her young family was broke. They had gotten behind in their bills and were finally evicted from their apartment for failing to pay $75 in overdue heating charges. They were homeless.

The officers were convinced she wasn't using meth. But they knew she was walking too close to the flames. "You get out of here, and get out of here now," a detective told her. "And don't come back."

She nodded. The officer wanted to make clear what was at stake. "Listen to me," the cop said. "We come back here, and find you here, we'll see that your kids are taken away from you. Do you understand?"

Yes, she promised. She would go right now. She threw some belongings into a couple of plastic clothesbaskets and loaded her car, a rusted rattletrap that looked like it had been retrieved from a junkyard. Then she pulled her kids along with her and loaded them into the car.

"Hey," officer John called out, asking her to wait for a moment. The tough-talking cop reached into the pocket of his jeans and pulled out $100 and handed it to her.

"Go pay your heat bill," he said. "And don't ever come back here."

CHAPTER THREE

"Works Just as Advertised": Women and Meth

When the social worker appeared at the door, Kaitlyn hid upstairs with her two-month-old son, Alex. "She's not here," a friend lied for her. "She's at Wal-Mart."

Kaitlyn peeked out the window of the apartment in the little Wisconsin town. She saw the social worker go back to her car, sitting and waiting. Down the street, a police officer sat in a parked squad car. Kaitlyn paced. She cried. She looked back out the window. It was clear: they were not going to go away.

The troubled twenty-two-year-old mother of a newborn was in a panic. She knew her last drug test must have showed positive for meth. Now there was nowhere to hide. Feeling like a hunted animal, she quivered for thirty minutes. Finally there was a knock at the door. The social worker was back. This time the uniformed police officer was at the door, too.

"We know she's in here," the social worker demanded. "We need to talk to her—now."

Kaitlyn crept down the stairs, shamed and scared. She thought she might pass out. She was holding the baby in her arms.

The social worker looked at Kaitlyn and spoke plainly, as if reading from a book. "It's been decided that it's in the best interest of your child," she said, "to be taken into custody and placed with temporary foster care."

Kaitlyn collapsed to her knees. She shrieked uncontrollably, still cradling the baby. "Oh please, please, give me one more chance," she sobbed. "Don't take my baby away." But a flood of tears would not change the reality. No matter how much she might love her child—and she did so love him—Kaitlyn knew the day of reckoning had come. She was an unfit mother. She had lost her baby to meth.

Once known as a drug for the blue-collar man, meth has become nearly as popular among women: teenage girls who want to party or cure the blues; mothers at home with kids; women working long hours at tedious jobs. Nearly half of all meth addicts now entering state treatment centers are women. Among cocaine or heroin abusers, men outnumber women two to one. But meth has special appeal for women. In a culture that worships women with skinny bodies, meth is the magic diet that finally works. With meth, the pounds run off like water. Women who never dreamed of fitting into a size four can slip into that little dress in a few months. Suddenly, the heads of men are turning. Men who never before seemed to notice or care are now walking across the room and saying hello. They want to know your name. They want your number. They want you. Even an Illinois beauty pageant contestant, a young woman who could scarcely be called overweight by any standards, started using meth to stay trim for the judges. She won a crown, but eventually lost much more.

And then there's the energy—the lift just when you need it. Meth makes it possible to clean the house, wash the clothes, fix the meals, tend to the kids—all on your spare time from working a job. Standing on your feet for hours on an assembly line, or as a waitress in a diner, can get so exhausting a woman can nearly drop. A little meth changes all that.

It changes your attitude, too. Women who felt themselves inadequate—homely or shy or not quite smart enough—all of a sudden gain some confidence. Women who have struggled with depression finally feel like they have the power to take on the world. In a romantic relationship, meth can heighten the sex drive and take away the old inhibitions. A woman can be more sexually adventurous for a husband or a boyfriend.

"For women, the benefits at first seem amazing: you lose weight, you've got all this energy, and then there's the euphoria," said Glen Hanson, the former head of the National Institute on Drug Abuse. "You feel like you're on top of the world."

In the beginning, many women—as well as men—do not even view meth as an intoxicant, but rather as an energy supplement, similar to the way some young athletes look at steroids. They are simply trying to find a way to be more possessed and productive.

"They often don't see it as a drug at first," said Susan Dreisbach, one of the authors of a recent study of meth users in Colorado. "A woman might be at work talking about feeling exhausted and a co-worker says, 'Hey, I've got just the thing to pull you through,' and slips a little meth into her pocket. Or maybe she's talking to a friend about depression, and the friend says, 'Hey, I know exactly what'll make you feel better.' And it's meth. And so they take it and bang, it works just like adver- tised. We really shouldn't be so surprised that people would be vulnerable to something like this. You know, we sort of live in this Starbucks culture. Is it really good to have twelve cups of espresso a day?"

Use for women tends to be sporadic and low-dose in the beginning, according to the study by Dreisbach and other re- searchers at the University of Colorado in Denver. "Nobody says, 'I started using this stuff because I intended to end up a junkie,'" she said. "The reality is that the addiction is so powerful that it creeps up on them, and it becomes a normal daily need."

For some women, it was a feeling of sadness and lethargy that led them to use meth, in hopes that it would shake them out of the doldrums. "Many people with depression will self- medicate with meth. They find, at first, that meth is a way to cope. Eventually, of course, it only makes the depression so much worse."

Much of the time, women on meth fall into abusive or con- trolling relationships with men who are also on meth. Some women become almost captives to the men and convince them- selves the relationship is built on love, when, more often than not, meth is the only thread the keeps them together. Women who get caught up with meth usually suffer poor self-esteem. That only gets worse as the meth takes its toll, and their sense of self-worth goes to tatters. Domestic violence is especially common in these situations. A man driven to paranoia by meth can go wild with rage that a wife or girlfriend is cheating or lying, and he may beat her senseless. Or he will try to control her every move, worried that she might go to the authorities and reveal the illegal drug use. In some cases, women on meth move from man to man, almost always in unhealthy relationships. Or they become so desperate for the money to get the drug that they sell their bodies on the street.

If the women decide they want help, finding it can be difficult. In rural areas, where meth is most pervasive, psychologists and counselors tend to be in short supply. In many of these small towns, social life revolves around church activities. For women who aren't comfortable with church, there are few other options for socializing or finding a support group. The social mores in small towns are usually conservative, and perhaps more judgmental about people who use drugs. In these settings, women are wary about sharing their problems or asking for help because they fear they will become outcasts. If social services are available, they are afraid they will bump into somebody they know along the way, since small towns lack anonymity. Women with children are afraid to share the truth about their meth addictions because they fear their kids will be taken away.

Meth use among women can often go undetected longer than it can for men, partly because women don't seem to "look" like the stereotype of criminals or drug addicts. This is especially true for women who spend most of their time at home. The addiction to meth among women is usually discovered only after something terrible has happened: when they commit crimes, neglect children, or give birth to babies who test positive for meth.

Kaitlyn, blond and blue-eyed, first tried meth in her little town in Wisconsin. She'd met a neighbor, a handsome young man named Matt. Months before that, she had gone through a serious bout of depression that put her in the hospital. She had dropped out of school and was spending her time just trying to cope. She had been living with her mother in an apartment.

But her mom, who struggled with illegal drugs and prescription painkillers, moved out, leaving Kaitlyn alone. In Matt, she had something—and someone—to live for. At first, she and the young man spent time taking walks around the lake, driving the country roads, and watching rented movies at home. Then one afternoon, when she stopped at his apartment, Kaitlyn found him sitting with a group of friends, listening to hard rock music on the radio, drinking beer, and smoking something through a straw.

"What's that?" she asked.

"It's meth," they told her. "Want to try some?"

Following their lead, she burned a lighter under a piece of tinfoil that held a little rock of the drug, inhaling the smoke through a straw. That afternoon, she smoked eight or ten or twelve times. She can't remember for sure how many. It gave her a burst of energy. "It made me feel cool," she said.

Kaitlyn went home that night and felt feverish and sick to her stomach. She finally went to bed and was able, after twisting and turning, to get some sleep.

It seemed like a risky thing to do. "But he was older, and I liked him," she said, "so I didn't think much about it."

The next week, they smoked meth again. It soon became a weekly ritual for them. "Over time, I wouldn't get so sick," she said. "I just got this great adrenalin rush." Then she moved into her boyfriend's condominium.

Before long, they were snorting meth with friends even more. The once-a-week habit turned to twice a week, then three times a week. It was costing more than $100 a week. Kaitlyn was working at a gas station, but her boyfriend, whose father owned a landscaping firm, made good money working in his family's business.

But the drug was starting to take its toll on both of them.

Kaitlyn got laid off from her gas station job because she was undependable. She lived on unemployment payments for a while, then she went to work for her dad's tire business. By then, she and Matt were smoking or snorting meth almost every day. And he was drinking heavily.

Kaitlyn would show up late for work, or not at all. She came to the job high, and she even smoked meth in the bathroom at her dad's business. She thought nobody noticed. She learned otherwise when her dad laid her off.

Soon she and Matt were using meth every chance they could. A friend who was a drug dealer introduced them to a purer, more potent form of meth called "glass." It was so strong that it burned her nostrils if she snorted it. But when she smoked it, the high was wonderful. "The high was just euphoric," she said. "You felt invulnerable. You didn't think about any bad things."

Kaitlyn and Matt lived for nothing else. They withdrew from friends and relatives. They stopped paying their bills. Finally, the bank foreclosed on Matt's condominium. With nowhere else to go, they moved into a camper next to Matt's dad's house. Everything was going down the drain. But it didn't matter. They wanted meth. They wanted it all the time.

On meth, sex with Matt seemed unbelievably good. "You just want to have sex all the time," she said. When they made love, he could last for hours. It was like magic. But suddenly the meth started playing tricks on his mind. "He'd see shadows and get paranoid," she said. "He'd hear a noise and think there were people in the attic."

And then he turned on her.

"He became really possessive," she said. "He'd get angry and accuse me of being with other guys. He wouldn't want me out of his sight."

For her part, Kaitlyn was shriveling. She weighed only ninety pounds. Her eyes were shrunken. Then she felt something strange about her body. She missed a period. She bought a pregnancy test. It was positive.

When she went to the clinic to confirm the pregnancy, the doctor threw her off guard with a question: "Are you taking drugs?" She denied it. But it worried her that the doctor could tell something was wrong with her just from looking at her. She and Matt decided it was time to clean up. They had a baby on the way. They vowed to stay away from meth. They stayed straight for about a month.

Back on the drug, Matt's delusions grew worse, and so did his temper. He was constantly accusing her of cheating on him.

"It's not my baby," he stormed.

"You're being ridiculous," she told him. "Of course it is." But the rants became more frequent, and more dangerous.

He'd push her around and corner her as he berated her. He'd slap her in the face.

She decided she needed to part from Matt. She moved in with a friend of theirs. Unfortunately, the friend was a drug dealer. Surrounded by drugs all the time, she was high more than she was sober. She worried the police would come and arrest her. She worried that she was doing serious damage to her baby. She couldn't stop using the meth, but she knew she had to get out.

One day, she called Matt and asked him to come and get her. "You've got to get me out of here," she said. "I'm so scared." Matt arrived almost immediately with his father. They gathered her belongings and moved her out of the drug dealer's place. Once more, she settled into the camper with Matt next to his dad's place. They smoked meth and tried to ignore the world— including the fact that she was now five months pregnant.

Just days after she moved back with Matt, they were walking near his dad's place when they noticed his pickup truck parked in an odd way. Something seemed strange. They walked near the truck and saw Matt's dad slumped forward against the steering wheel. Then they noticed the window next to his head was shattered. Matt's dad had shot himself to death. "We screamed as loud as people could scream," she said. Matt's father had suffered from depression. Matt and Kaitlyn could only wonder, but never know, how much their drug troubles had added to his sense of despair.

At the visitation and the funeral, Kaitlyn and Matt were as high as a kite. Matt's father had always been there to rescue them. After his father's suicide, Matt careened even further over the edge. Drunk and high on meth, he led police on a chase. When the cops caught up with him, he was standing on his mother's front lawn, throwing outdoor furniture around like a crazy man. The cops arrested him, took him for a drug test—it was positive, of course—and booked him on several charges. He spent a short stretch in jail.

As soon as he was free, he went straight back to meth. The paranoia and abuse grew worse. Kaitlyn decided to leave him again. Feeling as if she had nowhere else to turn, she moved once more to the apartment of their friend, the drug dealer. Kaitlyn told herself that she couldn't go to her dad's place because he would realize how terrible her drug problem had become, and she would be ashamed. But in truth, there was another reason: she wasn't ready to quit using meth. Before long, Matt was staying at the drug dealer's apartment, too.

Instead of seeing the drug dealer as part of the problem, they thought he was their safety net. He gave them a place to live. He gave them food. And he gave them meth for free—as much as they wanted. And they wanted plenty.

Eight months into her pregnancy, Kaitlyn went into labor in

the drug dealer's apartment. Just the night before, she had been smoking meth for hours. She knew she needed to go to a hospital, but she was too scared. She was afraid they could tell something was wrong with her. She was afraid there would be something terribly wrong with the baby. The meth had been able to block out reality before. But this time the harsh truth seemed inescapable.

She sat in a bathtub and cried. Nearly twenty-four hours passed, and the contractions grew stronger and stronger. The pain grew so intense Kaitlyn thought she might die. When she could not take it anymore, Kaitlyn and Matt asked their friend to drive them to the hospital. In terrible agony, Kaitlyn curled up in the car as it sped to the hospital. When the car pulled up at the hospital, the friend let them out at the curb and then rushed away.

Kaitlyn was barely able to walk, so Matt helped her into the hospital building. Nurses in the hallway could see it was urgent, so they put her in a wheelchair and rushed her to a delivery room. Within an hour, she gave birth to a baby boy. She was still high on meth.

The baby weighed five pounds and thirteen ounces, and the doctors said he seemed healthy. "I had been so worried that there would be something wrong with the baby," she said. She thought to herself, "It's a miracle." As far as she knew, the doctors were unaware that she was on the drug. She thought she was fooling them. But they knew something was terribly wrong. They asked her to save the baby's first diaper. Little did she know, they were testing the soiled diaper for meth.

The tests would take days. Kaitlyn was released with the baby, but she was told to come back for a checkup in a week. When she went home, she and Matt vowed to stay straight. "I had my baby, and I knew I had to stop using," she said.

The next week, she went to the clinic for the baby's checkup and was taken to a room where she waited for the doctor. When he came in, he closed the door and turned to her. It seemed his eyes were staring through her soul. "He had this look on his face," she said, "and he said, 'This is very serious—we've got to talk.'"

The doctor told Kaitlyn that meth had showed in the baby's system. He said the authorities might need to take the baby away from her. Kaitlyn collapsed on the floor in sobs, pleading for him to give her one more chance. The doctor told her she could keep the baby, but she would be visited by a caseworker, and random tests would be administered to make sure she was staying clean. He told her that while the baby seemed healthy for now, there were no guarantees. And he said the baby simply wouldn't be safe living with a mom who continued to use meth. Child welfare authorities, who were alerted by the doctor, could have moved to take Kaitlyn's baby away from her immediately. But they have discretion to give a mother a chance to clean up while they monitor her and test for drugs. They gave Kaitlyn that chance.

Kaitlyn went home and vowed to stay away from meth. Sober for the first time in years, she started to feel healthy again. She was eating better and finally managing to get some sleep. The baby was giving her a reason to live. She was feeling good about herself and believing that she could be a good mother.

Every week or so, the caseworker would come and take a test. Kaitlyn was clean. But her feeling of triumph in beating meth gave her a false sense of confidence. Off meth for a month, she began to believe that she had the power to take meth or leave it. "I thought, I really can leave this stuff alone when I want—so maybe it wouldn't hurt to do it just once more." She got high, promising herself not to touch the stuff again. But the next day, she smoked it again—and then the day after that.

On a Friday, the caseworker paid a surprise visit to Kaitlyn and asked her to provide a urine specimen. The young mother trembled with fear that she would be discovered. All weekend, she cried and fretted over what would happen next. The first thing on Monday morning, the caseworker was at the door, and Kaitlyn knew why. The tests had been positive. This time, her begging did not save her. The authorities gave Kaitlyn a few moments to pack up the baby's belongings—his blankie, his booties, his pajamas—and to say good-bye to him. She was told a court date would be set right away to determine what would be done with her baby. A hearing was held the next morning; the judge ruled that Kaitlyn's baby should go to foster care.

A pregnant woman using meth can pose serious harm for a baby. It's yet unclear just how serious those problems can be. Since meth has only recently emerged as a national scourge, there remains a dearth of medical studies about what the drug does to babies who are exposed to it. But medical experts already know that children of meth-abusing moms are more likely to be born premature and with low birth weight. In the worst cases, babies have a stroke and die or suffer permanent brain damage. In many hospitals today, doctors and nurses report delivering babies who are "jittery" and have problems eating. Sometimes the skin of the infant is tough or hardened. Dr. Rizwan Shah, a pediatrician at Blank Children's Hospital in Des Moines, Iowa, delivered her first meth-exposed baby in 1993. Since then, she has seen more than five hundred babies and young children who have been affected by the drug. One of her patients, a two-year-old boy, must be fed through a tube in his stomach because exposure to meth has left him unable to swallow properly. The prognoses of these babies can vary widely, and some of these kids can grow to adulthood without experiencing apparent problems.

Scientists have exposed rats to meth in the uterus and found the rodents were prone to eye defects, growth retardation, and delayed motor development. A Swedish study of children whose mothers had used amphetamines while pregnant found problems, as the kids grew older, including overly aggressive behavior, attention deficit problems, and lower achievement in academics and sports.

The harm caused by meth dominates the practice of Cheryll Jones, a pediatric nurse in Ottumwa, Iowa, who specializes in kids with severe health problems. When she started her practice in the 1980s in this Corn Belt town, she mostly saw kids with cerebral palsy, Down syndrome, or brain injury. "If somebody had told me twenty years ago that my practice would be mostly kids exposed to drugs, I'd have said they were crazy," she said. But that's mostly what she sees now. She says the problems don't fit a pattern that's easy to chart. "Some babies won't want to take an ounce of milk in an hour," she said, "and then there are those who can't stop themselves from eating; it's all they want to do."

One of her patients, a child of nearly three who was exposed to meth in the womb, cannot sleep for more than five hours a day. "And when he does go to sleep, it's not a good sleep." Some of the babies are so nerve-racked that doctors must prescribe sedatives to help them relax and sleep. The nursing staff uses infant massage to try to soothe them.

Exposure to meth has left some toddlers with extreme impulsivity problems. "We've got a four-and-a-half-year-old that you can't leave alone for a moment," she said, "or he'll get into something and get hurt because he just can't control himself."

Other kids have problems with aggression, such as toddlers who grow angry and want to lash out constantly. Some of the children have severe delays in learning to speak and then struggle in class when they enter school. Jones sees kids raised around meth labs who have serious respiratory problems or who have developed asthma that she suspects is related to exposure to the drug.

But these children can often recover. "These are not doomed kids," Jones stresses. "And we shouldn't look at them as hopeless causes. But they have some problems." As these kids get older, she said, many of them have extreme problems with organization. They start an activity, then turn away and start another. These aren't the usual distractible kids. These are children who seem frenetic. The problems suffered by meth-affected babies can get even worse if the parent continues to use the drug. Physical and sexual abuse of children is rampant with meth. Jones recites the grim litany: "Bruises, skull fractures, broken ribs, broken arms, shaken baby syndrome . . . it goes on and on."

In most states, child welfare agencies can do little to protect the fetuses of drug-using mothers. Child protection agencies only deal with kids who have been harmed. As one counselor put it, "They only step in after the bruise, not before." Authorities enter the picture only after a child has been born and has tested positive for meth or other drugs, or if the mother continues to use drugs.

But in Minnesota, a state-funded program called Project Child is devoted to finding pregnant women on meth and other drugs and trying to get help for them before they give birth and risk losing custody. Doctors, or sometimes probation officers, contact Project Child with information about a pregnant woman

who is using drugs, and then caseworkers approa
times on the street.

Kelly Krodel, one of the counselors who worl
nant addicts in the Minneapolis region, said a hig
of them turn to prostitution to feed their habit. Some of them
are turning tricks far into their pregnancy. The men who pay
them do not seem to care that they are sick and pregnant. "I've
had women tell me they get more customers when they're eight
months pregnant than when they're not showing," she said.
She has walked the streets to find some of these women, even
as they are soliciting customers.

"I've seen women on a street corner looking for a guy," she
said. "I've yelled, 'Get back here!' But then I watch her get into
a car with some guy—and they're gone."

When Project Child first started, some obstetricians were reluctant to make a notification about a pregnant woman using
drugs. They were afraid these women would recoil at the scru-
tiny and cease going in for prenatal health care. In reality, many
pregnant women express relief that they've been discovered,
that they no longer need to harbor the secret, and that someone is out there to help them, not punish them.

Krodel said she has yet to meet a pregnant woman using
drugs who doesn't really want to stop. At a visit with a twenty-
six-year-old in the woman's home, she sat down and smiled and
introduced herself. "You're not in trouble," she told her. "I want
to help you. I know you want to stop using. I know you want
to have a healthy baby."

She touched the woman's arm gently. "How much are you
using?" The woman, who was in the first trimester of her pregnancy, said she was taking more than three grams a day. The
pregnant woman looked frighteningly skinny. Her eyes were
hollow. She said she hadn't slept in seven days.

The counselor grasped her hand and asked her to walk to a mirror. "Look at yourself," Krodel said. "You look terrible."

The woman started to cry. "What do I need to do?" she asked, sobbing, as Krodel wrapped her arms around her.

"You need to get treatment," Krodel told her. "I'm going to call and find a place for you to go." She asked her when she could go.

"Right now," the pregnant woman replied.

The woman entered a twenty-one-day residential treatment program. The counselor visited her regularly, sometimes three times a week. They also talked frequently on the telephone. From the first visit, the counselor made clear what was at stake if the woman continued using meth. "If you keep using, your baby could have a stroke and die," she told her. "It could be born with birth defects. Or it might seem normal, and then struggle in school." She also told her straight about the legal consequences. "If you test positive when you give birth, child welfare will be there at your bedside. You will have to go to court. I might have to have you committed. And you might lose your baby."

Many of these women do lose their babies. "A lot of women don't make it, often because they don't have any family support," Krodel said. "Sometimes, that's a good thing. A baby can't be living from car to car, while her mother's prostituting."

But this twenty-six-year-old woman seemed determined to clean up. It helps that the social worker isn't judgmental. It also helps that she's been there herself. Krodel tells the woman about her own meth addiction.

"I used to use crystal meth," she told her. "I used to look like you. When I went into treatment, I weighed ninety-eight pounds. Now I've been clean for nineteen years—and you can get clean, too."

As Krodel knew, it wouldn't be easy for the woman, even after treatment. "If you feel like using, call me," she told her.

And the woman would call many times, saying, "I'm going to use—I'm in so much pain, I'm depressed, I can't do it. I don't want to go on like this."

Krodel would tell her to "think it all the way through" when considering taking meth. "Don't just think about getting high and what that will feel like. Think about what will happen afterward. Things will fall apart. Think about how you'll feel then. Think about the depression. Think about the way you'll worry about the health of your baby, about whether you'll lose this baby. But you've made it this far. You can do it."

Each time Krodel visited the woman's house, she could see improvement. Over time, she saw her make her house livable, bit by bit. "She took down the sheets that had been nailed over the windows. Then the place got cleaner. There was food in the refrigerator. The beds were getting made. She was gaining control of the place. She was making the house into a home." The twenty-six-year-old stayed clean. She gave birth to a healthy girl. It was a triumph of hope over pain. When she went home with the little girl, Krodel soon followed. Project Child continues to visit and monitor the recovering addict for several months after a child is born. The counselor knew relapse was always a possibility. They had plenty of long, agonizing, edge-of-the-cliff phone calls. "There were some close calls," Krodel said. "But she's stayed clean."

In working with these troubled women, Krodel knows that she can expect plenty of anger. Some of the women have screamed and cursed at her. They've told her she didn't understand their plight. They've told her they hated her. But down the road, many of these women have made the trip back to her office, clean and sober, and thanked her for saving their lives.

When Kaitlyn lost her baby to foster care, she drove to her dad's house in panic and desperation. He's a recovering alcoholic who has been sober for years. "I knocked on my dad's door, and I told him what had happened, that the baby had been taken away from me," she said. "I was so ashamed."

She didn't know how her father would react. Would he turn his back? Would he scorn her? Instead, he wrapped his arms around her and drew her near. "You need help," he told his weeping daughter. "It's not you. It's addiction. I've been there."

Her dad told her to gather her belongings and move in with him immediately. A week later, she moved into a treatment center in northern Wisconsin, the same place her father had gone to fight his war with alcohol. She was in residential treatment for sixty days. Her roommate was an alcoholic in her forties. There were sixteen people in treatment together. The youngest was an eighteen-year-old girl. The oldest was a man in his seventies. He was addicted to meth.

Kaitlyn's baby had been placed in a foster home with a family in her hometown. In treatment, she kept a pair of his pajamas and one of his blankets in her room with her, so that she could smell his scent and clutch at something of his. She covered the walls with photographs of her boy. During the day, she could scarcely think of anything but the baby. At night, she cried into the pillow until she fell asleep. "I was going through withdrawal from my baby," she said. "I was determined that I was going to do anything—absolutely anything—that I had to do to get him back."

She lived for the day, once a week, when the baby would be brought to her for a few hours. Under supervision, she was allowed to hold him, cuddle him, coo at him. When the precious minutes were up and it was time for the baby to be taken back to foster care, Kaitlyn would resist letting him out of her arms. "I broke down," she said. "I didn't want to give him back."

When she completed treatment, Kaitlyn moved back in with

her dad. Meanwhile, her baby's father, Matt, had quit using meth and was regularly attending Narcotics Anonymous and Alcoholics Anonymous meetings. He soon moved in with Kaitlyn and her dad. It was a little strange at first for the two of them to be together, Kaitlyn said, since they'd never known one another as sober people. "It was all kind of new to us," she said.

Before getting clean, meth had taken everything from Matt. He'd lost Kaitlyn and the baby. His condominium was foreclosed by the bank because he didn't pay the mortgage. He could have taken over his father's successful landscaping business after his dad died, but he was too strung out and broke to make it happen. The business and the equipment was auctioned off. "I had watched everything that I care about disappear," he said. When he quit using meth, the only job Matt could get was in a low-paying factory. But it was a start. He knew he wasn't going back to meth. "Everything changed when I held the baby in my arms," he said.

To get the baby back, Kaitlyn had agreed to submit to regular urine checks for meth and home visits from the caseworker. The goal was to "transition" the baby back to his mom, as long as she stayed clean. At first, she got to keep him for several hours. Then it was an entire night. And then it was two days a week. On the calendar on the wall in the kitchen, Kaitlyn and Matt marked off each day as getting one step closer to having the baby back. They drew a big circle around March 25, the day when he would be back for good. When that day came, Kaitlyn felt a sense of peace that she had never known before. The baby is now a year and a half old, smiling and babbling and playing. He looks healthy and happy. It seems almost too good to be true. Kaitlyn and Matt hope and pray that he continues to be healthy. They know how fortunate they have been, and they thank God every single day that they—and the baby—seem to have been blessed by grace.

Matt recently got a good job as a heavy-equipment operator. It pays a good wage. He gets laid off in the winter months, since it's too cold to dig. But that works out well for him and Kaitlyn. It gives him a chance to stay home with the baby while Kaitlyn goes to school. Matt says he loves nothing more than to spend hours playing with his little boy. He can't wait to take his son fishing someday soon. He loves being a dad and vows to be a good one. "I only wish my dad could see me now," he says. He knows his father would be proud of the way he's turned his life around.

Kaitlyn has enrolled in college to become a nurse. She wants to work in the pediatric department because she loves babies so much. She's still working hard on recovery, a process she knows will last a lifetime. She goes to Twelve Step meetings every Monday, Tuesday, Thursday, Friday, and Saturday. On some days, she goes more than once. She also volunteers at the local jail, mostly talking to young women who have become addicted to meth or other drugs. Many of them have had their babies taken away from them. "I tell them what I've been through, and I ask them what they've been through," she says. "Most of all, I tell them there's hope."

CHAPTER FOUR

Nobody's in Charge but Meth

The highway was too busy to cross on foot safely. But the two little Iowa kids decided to make a run for it. They were brother and sister, on a mission for survival. He was seven. She was five. Their clothes were tattered and filthy. Their hair was greasy. Dirt was caked under their fingernails. But all these children could think about was food. They weren't just hungry. They were starving. It had been days since they'd been fed. There wasn't a morsel of food in their house, and their parents were zonked—sleeping off a meth binge. From their front yard, the kids could see a convenience store on the other side of State Highway 34. They decided to go there and see if they could get something to eat. It would be scary, but they saw no other choice. With cars zooming from both directions, they held hands and then scampered as fast as their little legs could carry them. They made it. Still huffing, the kids walked through the parking lot to the entrance of the store. It hadn't occurred to these kids that they would need money, though, and their pockets were empty. So they stood outside the store, shivering in the raw wind that raked the prairie, and begged people for a dollar or two, enough to get a candy bar.

"When we go into a house where meth is being used, the first thing we do is check the refrigerator," said Marvin Van Haaften, the Iowa drug czar. "You look in there, and maybe you'll find some mason jars for meth oil. But you won't find milk or eggs or bread. There's absolutely nothing to eat. Sometimes you look in the fridge and there's nothing but mold."

In these homes, nobody's in charge but meth. It rules all. The drug so jumbles the mind of an addict that it's nearly impossible to see through the fog of everyday life. Trying to run a household while on meth is like trying to decipher a mysterious code. Nothing makes sense. The drug plays such tricks with the brain that imaginary voices seem to scream and real ones go unheard. These people do not stop loving their children. They are trapped and lost. For as long as they can, they have summoned the will to press ahead. But in time, theirs becomes the role of Sisyphus, and meth the unmovable stone.

For children living with parents on meth, going hungry is just part of the bargain. Meth users don't eat because they don't get hungry, so they often forget that their kids need food. Malnourishment is just one of the problems endured by kids growing up around meth, and it's one of the more benign ones. In the worst cases, children are beaten by meth users filled with rage or hallucinations, or they're sexually abused by addicts so charged up with carnal desire they foist themselves on whoever happens to be around, no matter that they're not old enough to drive or, in some cases, old enough to be in kindergarten. Children in meth-fueled homes live in an insane asylum—and the inmates really are in charge. In some cases, no one is in charge, except perhaps an older sibling, and kids are left to fend for themselves, so neglected they must run across a busy highway in a desperate search for food. The little kids who raced across Highway 34 and begged for food wound up in the hands of child welfare authorities and were ultimately placed in foster care.

Since 1995, in Iowa alone more than 1,000 children have been present at meth labs during police arrests. More than 1,400 kids in the state who are living with parents who use the drug have tested positive for meth. These are not adolescents using the substance, but kids who have been poisoned from living with the fumes or unwittingly ingesting it, literally, hand-to-mouth. "And we know that that's just the tip of the iceberg," Van Haaften said. "There are so many more out there we don't know about."

Van Haaften, the former sheriff of Marion County, has seen kids endure horrors worse than any nightmare. "Meth has affected the citizens of Iowa like nothing else ever has," he said. "For the children, it's a form of torture." In one case, Van Haaften found a two-and-a-half-year-old and a four-year-old living with their meth-addicted dad—the mother was in jail on meth charges—and neither child knew how to drink from a cup. Neither had been toilet trained. Their teeth were rotting. They had almost no language skills. Van Haaften has seen homes where the garbage hadn't been taken out in months, and gnats and flies were so thick that the police camera couldn't focus properly. He has walked through a meth-using home where there was no toilet paper and the adults were using the kids' clothes to wipe themselves. "That's where meth will leave you," he said.

In some homes, every cupboard hinge and door handle is corroded with white powder from meth. "It makes you wonder what the lungs of small children around this look like," Van Haaften said. In one case, a small girl sat in a car while her parents cooked and drove around with the windows down to get rid of the smell. In another, an infant who drank from a baby bottle used to mix meth ingredients was taken to the hospital and lingered for a time in critical condition. The baby lived, but it's impossible to know what problems will develop later from having drunk the residue. Another child exposed to meth fumes was hospitalized with a life-threatening illness from the toxins. Police once discovered a two-and-a-half-year-old girl in a severely lethargic condition. It turned out she was sickened after licking a spoon the parents used while making meth. Still another child, a ten-month-old, was discovered having seizures in a meth lab and was rushed to the hospital.

It's not just the drug itself, but also the parents or other adults in the home who are high on meth that can cause monstrous consequences for children. One child in Iowa was savagely beaten to death in a home where his mother and her boyfriend were using meth. Police believe the boyfriend went on a meth-induced rage and pounded the baby until his breathing stopped and his heart was still. The man was acquitted of murder charges, but the case gave rise to a new law, nicknamed the Boyfriend Bill. The law allows for child endangerment charges to be brought against not just the parents or legal guardians, but "any adult who has control" over a minor.

One man left his young son in a bathtub while he smoked the drug in the living room, too high to realize the danger. When the dad finally went back to check on his son, the baby had drowned in the tub. After a flash fire triggered by a meth lab badly burned a man's young son, the father, fearful of being discovered as a meth cook, did not take his son to a doctor for days. The child, meanwhile, was left to endure excruciating pain. When he was finally taken to the hospital, not much could be done to ameliorate the damage done by the burns, so the child will live with gruesome scars. Other children have been sexually abused by a meth-addled parent or another adult, some as young as toddlers. After the assault, some children are left infected with sexually transmitted diseases.

Besides enduring the neglect, and sometimes the horror, children wander around homes that seem swept by a tornado, so chaotic they are nearly impossible to navigate. The television blares all night, and crashing parents sometimes sleep all day. Piles are everywhere: clothes, newspapers, food wrappers. Nothing is where it should be, so trying to find a toy or a pair of shoes can be a futile search. But children do find some things that cannot help but shock them. It is common to find the meth itself in kids' rooms, or even hidden in cribs. Pornography is frequently discovered in bedrooms of the children. "And it's almost a given that a meth cook will have firearms just inside the door," Van Haaften said.

When drug task force teams move on a meth lab, they often check with the school to make sure the kids aren't at home, so they can be spared the traumatizing spectacle of their parents being busted. But it's not always possible. During one recent crackdown, young children fretted inside as they heard the police call out in loud voices that they were breaking inside the home. The kids heard and saw a big steel bar breaking down the door, followed by a SWAT team, guns pulled, charging into their home. "It's a terrible experience that these kids will never forget," said Van Haaften. "The kids will be crying, whimpering, moaning, lying face down on the floor."

One bust took place in the middle of the night, as children awoke to screaming and a confrontation between law enforcement and their parents. During one arrest, police walked into a house and were met by a five-year-old boy who immediately held his hands straight in the air. Authorities said the boy had been conditioned to "surrender" after seeing his father make the gesture so many times before. When children are removed from such dangerous homes and driven by police to child welfare authorities, they have been known to beg for protection. More than once, a child has wrapped his or her arms around an officer and squeezed tightly. Van Haaften said he's seen children ride to child welfare offices in the squad car who plead, "Please don't ever make me go home."

Besides the imminent dangers of living with people whacked out on meth and in homes that can literally be blown to pieces, many of the children of meth users run the risk of a legacy of problems, physical and psychological, that could haunt them years down the road in ways that no one today can gauge or predict. Just as it was for those who worked around asbestos, it might take decades before respiratory problems reveal themselves in those exposed to meth fumes. In the same vein, experts say learning or attention deficits might not become apparent among some of these children until well into elementary school. As for the psychological scars, it's hard to imagine a child ever forgetting some of the horrifying images engraved in their psyches: the sight of the empty, hollowed eyes of a mother or father stoned into lunacy; the sting of a lashing belt or cord as punishment for simply existing and being a burden to a worshipper of a drug; the unspeakable terror of feeling an unwelcome adult's hands, then his fingers, rushing down there, in that place, the most intimate invasion, and the sound of a zipper being unzipped, and the weight of a man—a greasy, smelly, crazy man—forcing himself on top of a petrified child trapped beneath. What will it take, child advocates are wondering, to heal from such wounds?

"We certainly need to make the initial rescue," said Van Haaften. "But we've got to do something more than just get them out of the house. These are not throwaway children.

They're resilient. But they're going to face some serious challenges. And we've got to make sure they get the help they need." The problems wrought by meth have burdened the foster care system as children are put in temporary homes, often to be shuttled from place to place. In other cases, grandparents or aunts and uncles step in to care for the neglected kids.

Health care professionals, meanwhile, work to heal children who lag behind their peers in some ways, and in other ways know far more than any child should know. When these kids reach the offices of pediatric nurse Cheryll Jones, myriad issues need to be addressed. These are children who have been parted from what semblance of family they have known. They have even lost their toys, since everything in a meth house needs to be decontaminated or thrown away. In some cases, Jones sees a condition known as "attachment disorder." These kids have never felt an emotional connection with anyone, nor have they grown to cultivate trust, because their caregivers have been psychologically or even physically absent much of their lives. "They've never bonded with anyone," said Jones, "so it's hard for them to empathize with anyone else's feelings." Some of these children are treated in play therapy, where they are taught how to socialize with other kids, catching up on skills like sharing and respecting boundaries.

Many of these kids are reluctant to open up to anyone. "Many of the kids are very suspicious of people," Jones said. "They've been conditioned by paranoia. They're taught to keep secrets and to never talk to people." For children who remain with parents, Jones said it is important to treat the entire family. "You can't just treat the child in isolation," said Jones. "You've got to try to get everyone healthy, or it won't work." In some cases, young children are very frank about their frustration and anger at what they've been through. Jones said she once examined a six-year-old while his meth-using mother stood in the room. The boy spoke plainly to his mom. "I'm really mad that you keep using drugs and you have to go to jail and I have to go to foster care," he told her. Other children talk about the meth-induced memory loss of their parents and their own feelings of loss. These kids will talk about major events in their past—school events, concerts, ball games—and their parents don't have a clue about these experiences. Jones knows that many people believe meth-abusing parents should be banished from the lives of their kids. "A lot of people out there say we should just take these kids away immediately and put all the parents in jail," she said. But losing a parent, however sick and flawed, can bring its own set of psychological problems for a child. These children suffer terrible grief, even guilt, that the relationship with a parent has been severed.

Children who are removed from parents frequently have a difficult time finding a niche in a new family. They are suddenly expected to assume a radically changed role. Growing up as they have, with parents who could not be counted upon even for the simplest things, many of these kids have grown accustomed to acting as the parents themselves. They were the ones who made sure that younger brothers and sisters woke up for school, got dressed, and got something to eat. They were the ones who went out and called younger siblings home when darkness fell in the evening and made sure the little ones found their way to their beds at night. "It's a real problem for these kids when they go to foster care because they've been used to being the caregivers—that was their role," Jones said. "Then all of a sudden that's taken away from them." Even as they grow older, these kids are haunted by sleep problems, not only because the darkness has come to be associated with terror, but also because their nervous systems have simply been damaged by exposure to meth. These are children whose minds and bodies simply cannot relax.

"There's a whole range of issues we're going to need to address with these kids, and we're just getting started," said Jones. "We've got to get together and figure out, 'Okay, folks, what are we going to do for these children?'" When Jones goes to medical conferences and talks about the problems in Iowa, people from other parts of the country seem astonished. "They'll say, 'When I think of Iowa, I think of farms and cows and tranquility,'" she said. "And I'll tell them, 'Yeah, we've got all those things. But we've got our problems, too.' The truth is, it's awfully easy to get lost out in rural Iowa."

The kids were afraid to talk to their mother, Anne, who was shooting meth into her body. She hit them. She swore at them. She screamed at them, "Just leave me alone!" They learned early not to speak their minds, or even to talk to her at all, if they could avoid it. "I was not a very nice mom," Anne said. With her children in the car, she would fly into a rage when another car cut her off in traffic, screaming and swearing. She once stopped the car in the middle of the road, looking for a fight with another driver. She took her kids with her to places where people were shooting meth, or she left them alone for long stretches while she took the drug or sold it.

Dad was out of the picture. He'd left a few years before, chasing meth parties and having sex with one woman after the next. Infidelity is almost a given with meth addiction. The revved-up libido is often just what men crave about the drug. Cheating doesn't mean they'll leave the house. But it can become more of a shelter and less of a home. Some fathers stay for the kids. But since they're usually the meth cooks, or at least the purchasers of the drug, the amount of time spent securing a drug supply doesn't leave much to spare for playing catch in the yard. The edginess and paranoia of meth use often leads them to berate their kids. For all that, it's usually better for the children to have Dad around than Mom's addicted boyfriend.

That's who Anne's three children had for a housemate. The boyfriend, a meth addict who stole anhydrous ammonia and cooked it, seemed to be exploding with venom. He spit in Anne's face. He slammed her against the wall. He chased her around the neighborhood with a knife. "The kids saw all of it," said Anne. Once, while he was beating their mom, the oldest daughter, who was about twelve, picked up the telephone and walked into the other room. She was trying to call the police without the boyfriend knowing about it. But when he realized that she was on the phone, he went into a rage. He slapped the phone out of her hands, then yanked the girl to the ground by her hair. "The kids lived with the fear that he was going to kill all of us," Anne said.

Everyone in the family was expected to keep secrets about the meth use. Anne tried to put up a good front. She took the kids fishing and camping. She went to parent-teacher conferences. She thought nobody knew what was going on in her life. She learned differently when her older daughter was told by a friend that she couldn't sleep over "because your mom is a drug dealer."

Anne ended up getting treatment and joining an Iowa group called Moms On Meth—the name was later changed to Moms Off Meth. In the group, women talk about how they became addicted to meth and what it has meant for them and for their children. The group started in 1999 in a small Iowa town with just four mothers in recovery. Now there are chapters across the state: Ottumwa, Keokuk, Centerville, Cedar Rapids, Fort

Dodge, and Albia, with one planned to open in Fairfield and others on the way. The meetings often attract twenty-five to thirty women. The meetings are off the record. No child welfare authorities are allowed to come in and take notes about what is being said. And everybody who comes does so freely. The group does not allow for attendance by court order. It is meant to be a supportive and safe place, perhaps the first safe place many of these women have known in a very long time.

Moms Off Meth was started by a woman named Judy, who kicked meth and won back the custody of her three children after twelve years of shooting the drug into her body. She had been a drug dealer who spent time in jail for stealing to support her habit. "There's so much guilt and shame," she said. "We try to send out a message of hope." Like many women, Judy, who has struggled with weight issues all her life, had started using the drug for its ability to make her thin and to help her feel attractive. "Meth is a very seductive drug," she said. "You take it and it tells you you're powerful and beautiful and smart. It gives you the feeling that you're worth something. You take it and you think, 'My God, this is the thing I've been looking for.'"

With the other women in the group, Judy shares her story of getting hooked on meth, loving it, and then hating it. "For years," she said, "I would cry and pray to die." She ran the gamut of meth-induced insanity. She took up with one boyfriend after the next, as her children watched her partners come and go. The kids had no structure and little guidance. She dealt the drug and "stole everything I could get my hands on" to trade for meth. Her story resonates with other women in the group. Many of them have lost their children because of meth. Still others explain how they succumbed to meth, again and again, even as they fought to get their kids back. In many cases, a visit to the kids in foster care—and the anguish of leaving them—plunged them into such despair that they turned to the only thing they knew of that could numb the pain: meth.

The women in the group talk about things they've kept bottled up for years: memories of being neglected and abused themselves as children. Some of the stories are harrowing. One woman recounted that, as a young girl, she would lie in bed and hear the dreaded, heavy footsteps of her father walking up the stairs. In the darkness, he would enter the room and drop his pants. Then he would force himself into the mouth of his daughter. After he was finally done, the girl would slip into the upstairs bathroom and brush her teeth for hours, trying to rinse away the terrible taste of abuse. Later, as a mom, she would "freak out" when her own daughter would brush her teeth. It brought back memories so traumatic that she trembled and wept. In meth, she looked for something that could erase the horrid visions of her own childhood and give her a sense of peace. Instead, it brought chaos. Some of the women were reared by alcoholics. Some grew up being demeaned and battered. Still others came from stable, two-parent, middle-class homes—the clichéd white-picket-fence Midwest—but ended up being swallowed by meth.

As leader of the group, Judy asks these women simply: "What's going on? How can we help?" Many of these women were in relationships where they were controlled, figuratively or literally, and were conditioned to think they needed permission to speak what was on their minds. In the meetings, they feel liberated at last to bare their souls, to vent, at times, and to dare to plan a better life for themselves. Sometimes it's a matter of listening to their sadness and anger—outrage that "the system" has taken their children, indignation that the fathers have simply skipped out on their responsibilities—and understanding the shame that comes with addiction. "We need to get to the solution now," Judy reminds them. "I don't think you're a bad mom. But your self-esteem has been beaten down."

As these women try to get their lives back on track, they can become overwhelmed by challenges like finding a job, caring for the kids if they still have them, and figuring out how to win them back if they don't. Judy found that simple things can make a big difference. She gives each woman an appointment book. It is a way to help them organize their lives and bring some sense of order to the whirlwind. She gives them daily meditations to read, simple words that bring a sense of peace. She urges them to keep a journal to write down their emotions, their fears, and their goals, and perhaps most of all, to give them a sense of control over their lives.

One of the chief goals of the group is talking about the triggers that can send them into relapse. One of the biggest issues is weight gain during recovery. "They'd say, 'I don't feel attractive. The guys just don't like you when you're fat. And I feel disgusting,'" said Judy. "And we'd tell them: 'This is a process. Your body has been starved for a long time. So you're naturally going to gain some weight.'" The group brings in nutritionists to talk about healthy ways to maintain weight and about how to exercise to burn calories and stay fit.

Trusting other women is also an obstacle for many of the mothers in recovery from meth. Because sexual promiscuity almost always comes with meth use, these are women who have bitter memories of husbands or boyfriends sleeping around, often with their friends or others in the drug circle. And since these groups are held in small towns in Iowa, sometimes "the other woman" is sitting right across the table. "It's not the easiest thing to be in the room with somebody that you know was sleeping with your boyfriend," said Judy. "So we talk a lot about how those are things that happen when you're using. It's the drug, not the person. And we talk a lot about forgiveness, for ourselves and for each other, and about getting on with things."

A big challenge for these women is figuring out how to build activities that mesh with a sober lifestyle. "Many of these women are afraid to be sober," Judy said. "They usually started using when they were very young. It's been such a long time for them. They don't know how they'll feel or act as sober people." At first, they're not even sure what to do with themselves. "When you've spent 90 percent of your time at home doing drugs, or going to the bars," Judy said, "you start to wonder to yourself: *What do sober people do?*" So the group plans a lot of activities that give the women a chance to spend time together, bond, and learn that having fun doesn't require drugs or booze. They have bake sales, slumber parties, car washes to raise money for charities, even trips to the amusement park. They talk about the importance of being around sober people and of going to places where people don't drink or use drugs.

More than anything, the mothers talk with anguish about how their meth use brought so much pain to their children, and the challenges they face in rearing their kids now that they have stopped using the drug. "There is tremendous guilt about what they've done to their kids while they were using," said Judy. "You tell them, 'Yeah, you did some bad things then. But you're not in that situation now.'" In recovery, parents often wake up to the reality that their children have been deeply affected by the addiction in ways that won't simply disappear once the drug is gone. Sometimes for the first time, these parents are hearing their children talk honestly about the addiction from their vantage: the nightmares about a mother getting hurt or lost or simply deciding not to come home; the feelings of disappointment when a parent doesn't show up at a game or a school concert, or shows up looking like a wreck; the resentment felt by kids for being forced to lie to people for years to hide the parent's drug use. Judy said the mothers are encouraged to speak candidly to the kids about the past. "You can say, 'I'm sorry—I know it had to be hard for you. I know you were frightened and angry and crazy about this. Do you want to talk about it?'" Earning back the trust of kids can take time. Every time a mother leaves the house, they cannot help but wonder if she's gone back to using the drug, and they question whether she's coming back home. Judy says her own children became anxiety-ridden every time she went to the bathroom, and they became angry when she closed or locked the door. "It's because the bathroom is where I went to do drugs," she said. "And even after I got sober, the kids would wonder: 'How long has she been in there? What's she really doing behind that door?'"

For the children, especially if they are older, there is often a difficult period of adjustment after a parent quits taking drugs. "When Mom gets sober, she wants to be Mom," said Judy. But the kids tend to resist the new rules that come with a sober parent. These are kids who have been accustomed to running wild and doing whatever they want, whenever they want. "There are often control issues with the kids," said Judy. "They don't like the change in power." One of the most difficult issues for sober moms comes when their own children start using drugs or alcohol. Many of these parents take for granted that if they stop using a substance, their children will avoid the pitfalls of alcohol and other drugs. It's usually a mistaken notion. These kids are likely to be as curious and daring as the next kid, as far as drugs are concerned. And they have a trump card to play. An adolescent who starts drinking or using drugs can always say indignantly: "How hypocritical of *you* to say I shouldn't use drugs or alcohol. *You, of all people!*"

Judy knows firsthand about that. Her son, who was four years old when she started using meth, began drinking as a teenager. She would ground him. But his drinking got worse, and then he got into drugs. She committed him to treatment. But when he got out, he went back to alcohol and drugs and got into trouble with the law. Before long, he was hooked on meth and went to jail. "I was devastated," said Judy. "I thought to myself: 'Look what I've caused.'" But her son simply had to fight the same war, in his own way, that his mother had waged. Now twenty-four, he's been through treatment again. He's in college now, and he's staying sober.

For Anne, there is no denying that her drug-using days took their toll on her kids. "For a long time, whenever I'd raise my voice, they'd get scared," she said, her voice still aching with re-gret, "because they remembered the way things were before." With shame, she talked again about the lying, the hitting, the neglect, as if she were repeating her sins in confession. "I think—no, I know—that my kids are still affected by my meth addiction." She talked again about her eldest being humiliated by hearing the town gossip about her mother being a druggie. The girl couldn't be blamed if she harbored some anger, resent-ment, and mistrust. That child had been put through some hell-ish times. But she had also seen the power of grace. Not long after Anne had been out of treatment, and was struggling to stay sober, her daughter came up to her mother to speak her mind. "Mom," she told her, out of the clear blue, "I'm so proud of you."

CHAPTER FIVE

The Poisoning of the Gay Community

Growing up in blue-collar Pennsylvania, where real men pounded nails and slammed beers, Thomas didn't feel as though he fit. From a very early age, he seemed drawn to a different path. There was a price to be paid for stepping out of line. He didn't have a lot of friends. Even his own father gave him a hard time. On a school trip to the library as a third grader, he checked out a piece of artwork and brought it home. His dad hit the roof. No red-blooded American boy should care about art! That was for sissies! Basketball and football—that's what should interest a boy. Thomas had tried sports. He'd stood in the line on the school playground as teams were divided for games. He was always picked last. At least that's how it seemed. He saw himself as a skinny runt. In truth, he really didn't care about sports. When he got to be nine or ten, he decided it was silly for him to pretend that they mattered to him. At a block party, when a bunch of other kids decided to play volleyball,

Thomas said he'd sit it out. It was no big deal. He just didn't feel like playing. But his dad fumed about his son's lack of interest in athletics. In front of everybody, he gave the boy a tongue-lashing and sent him home.

Thomas was accustomed to his father's tirades. They were especially wicked on Friday nights, when the man got drunk at the saloon after his shift was done and then stumbled in the door at home ready to declare war on anyone who got in his way. Thomas tried to stay clear of him, at least until the man passed out on the living-room couch. As his dad slept it off, young Thomas would try to keep very quiet. He knew that if his father woke, the trouble would start all over again. His father's bursts of temper frightened Thomas. It hurt enough that his father didn't seem to approve of him. But the flashes of temper genuinely scared him. In reality, it was his dad who was scared. Thomas figured it out many years later.

"I think he knew that I was gay even before I knew it," Thomas said. "He couldn't handle that."

As a sixteen-year-old, Thomas was caught by his mother kissing another boy in his bedroom at home. She told him he shouldn't do that. But the incident triggered no discussion about Thomas's sexuality. It was a testament to the remarkable powers of denial. Even Thomas, in the wake of passionately necking with another boy, did not dare consider the possibility that he was gay. In his household, outward appearances mattered more than anything else, but behind the perfectly manicured lawn existed a troubled family. Through high school and even college, Thomas engaged in a world of pretend. He told people at college that he came from a wealthy family with a summer home and even talked about extravagant vacations they had taken. When he got rides home from college mates, he had them drop him off in front of a big fancy house, instead of his own modest home, as part of the ruse. It was not until his early twenties that he acknowledged to himself that he was gay. He told his mother, who stressed that he not tell his dad. Thomas had finally come to terms with his sexuality, but even then he did not accept himself or his background, continuing to spin tales. "I hated myself so much that I reinvented who I was," he said later. "I didn't like the real me."

All that self-loathing seemed to vanish on the night he first snorted meth. At a party, he tried the drug at the urging of another man he liked. It burned his nostrils and his throat. But it also sent his confidence soaring. "I was like, 'Oh man—I'm on top of the world.' I had this rush of energy. I felt like I was ten times bigger. It was fabulous. I felt perfect." By the time he found meth, Thomas had become a successful financial analyst for an insurance company in New York. He met a man he loved and followed him to San Francisco, where he found an even better job. To Thomas, it seemed like he had found his place in the world. His career was zooming and he was in love. For the first time in his life, he felt like he had it all.

Meth didn't swallow Thomas right away. He used the drug three or four times a year at "circuit parties," exuberant all-night dance parties. These were lavish affairs held in big warehouses or mansions in Los Angeles, San Francisco, New York, Miami. Strobe lights splashed the dance floor in colors. Interesting men from around the country got to know each other intimately—if only for a few hours. The places seemed to pulsate with energy. And there was meth. "You could do meth and dance and stay up all night. You could have sex forever. It was pure hedonism. It was all about me."

Thomas was working for a Fortune 500 company, pulling down a six-figure income. He was living in a posh condo and driving a flashy imported car. But he couldn't wait for the circuit parties and the chance to do meth. It was too long to wait for such a good thing. Thomas and some friends started to do meth every now and then, and before long it was a weekend ritual. It seemed manageable enough. He showed up for work on time and excelled at his job. He was getting to the gym regularly and keeping himself looking buff. He was living proof, he told himself, that you could be a successful executive and a meth user. "I thought I had it under control," he said. "And then it turned on me."

Thomas decided he didn't need to wait until Friday to get high. Wasn't Thursday close enough to the weekend? Going without sleep for days, Monday mornings were starting to hit hard. He was so exhausted it was difficult to get out of bed to go to work. The only thing that could get him started was a little more meth. "I'd do a bump, and that'd get me going enough to go to work." It didn't take long until it was every day. In the end, he stopped going to work for long stretches, calling in sick with some trumped-up illness. He and his partner split, and Thomas started getting high on meth around the clock. His habit was costing $100 a day, and it threatened to cost him his life. "I felt trapped," he said. "I couldn't get out of bed without meth." He made it into work every now and then. Somehow, nobody seemed to notice how sick he had become, or at least nobody told him. "I kept my head down at work," he said, "but my life was completely emotionally unmanageable. The depression, the anxiety—I couldn't stand it. I felt like I was walking on the edge of a razor." In a stupor one night, Thomas used some tweezers to try to pull out a hair that may or may not have been on his face. He finally passed out.

When he woke the next morning, he looked in the mirror. What he saw shocked him. He had apparently gone berserk with the tweezers. There were gouges from his chin to his forehead, and almost everywhere in between. His face looked as if he had been slashed and beaten. He stared at the mirror in horror, then he heard a voice. This wasn't like the other voices of terror. This time it was different. It spoke the truth: "You finally look as ugly on the outside as you feel on the inside."

Thomas knew he needed help. He called the human resources department at his company to find out if his insurance would cover a visit to a treatment center. Thomas was one of the lucky ones. He had good insurance, and within a week, he was headed to a facility that specializes in treatment for gays and lesbians with drinking or drug problems. Before he got on the plane, he got higher than a kite. He even brought a vial on board to take a "bump" during the flight. He cried as he used the meth. Part of him was relieved that he was finally getting help. Another part of him was mourning the wreck he had become and feeling anxious about a new life without the drug. When he got off the plane, he took a cab to the treatment center, a low-slung brick building that looked like an elementary school. Across the street, he spotted a funeral home. The irony was not lost on him. It had become clear that he had two paths he could follow: he could get healthy, or he would die. In the treatment center, a counselor forced him to come to terms about what meth had done to his life. "I sobbed until my shirt was soaked with tears," he said. "I'm going to die someday. But I don't want to die of meth."

Not since the horrifying days of the AIDS crisis in the 1980s has anything so poisoned America's gay communities as methamphetamine has. For years, meth has been regarded as a plague of the rural hinterlands. But nowhere is the problem of meth any worse than in urban gay communities, or its consequences so devastating. In the gay neighborhoods of New York, such as

Chelsea, the drug is often known as "Tina." And it can be found in a Manhattan minute. "You couldn't throw a stick in Chelsea without hitting somebody that has a meth problem, or somebody who knows somebody who has one," said Dan Carlson, a founder of an antimeth group called HIV Forum. "Nobody can deny it anymore because it's become so obvious."

For gay men, the dangers of meth are manifold. People who inject the drug with dirty needles can acquire HIV. Meth-using gay men are more likely to have multiple sex partners, and they are much more likely to have anal intercourse without a condom, leaving them much more vulnerable to infection with the virus that causes AIDS. In a Los Angeles study of 1,600 men who reported having sex with other men in the last year, 13 percent acknowledged using meth. The meth users were twice as likely to report having unprotected sex and four times as likely to be HIV-positive. The Centers for Disease Control and Prevention estimates that men high on meth are four times more likely to have unsafe sex than men who aren't. Counselors at the Callen-Lorde Community Health Center in New York say as many as three-quarters of the new patients diagnosed with AIDS are telling them that meth played a role in their acquiring the virus. Meth use is also suspected in a sharp rise in syphilis in New York, often a harbinger of a growing rate of HIV infection.

Drug and alcohol problems do not discriminate based on sexual orientation. But it's a not-so-well-kept secret that the use of "recreational drugs" has long been an accepted feature of life in many gay communities. "People in the gay community may not like to hear it, but we are a chemically embracing culture," said Carlson. "Meth in particular is a very seductive drug for gay men. In a world where you don't feel very powerful, the high on meth—that feeling of invincibility—is a very appealing thing." It is all the more alluring to young men who have left small

towns—feeling beaten down and rejected for their sexuality—
and feel liberated in big cities. Counselors say these young men
see meth as a way to help them feel sexy and powerful in a way
they never had before.

Carlson said people trying to get the word out about the
dangers of meth have sometimes been met by fierce resistance.
"It's been considered heretical in the gay community to speak
out against drugs. Forty years ago, we couldn't even dance together. We've been held in a closet for so long that there's a
feeling that we don't like to be told what we can or should do.
We don't like the idea of rules being imposed on us. But enough
is enough. We need to take a look at who we are and what
we're about. We want to shatter the complacency and break the
silence around HIV and meth. We have to take care of each
other because nobody else is going to do it for us."

One gay official put it bluntly: "It's unreal the way this problem is being swept under the rug. It's the same kind of attitude
we first saw with AIDS. The problem is that a lot of the decision makers in our community are using this drug. These
people talk about 'harm reduction.' When it comes to crystal
meth, there is no moderation. It eats you up and spits you out."
It is difficult to estimate how many lives in the gay community
have been ruined by meth. "We're seeing cases nobody could
have imagined," said Carlson. "We're seeing people so paranoid
on meth that they can't leave their houses. We're seeing people
with million-dollar jobs end up homeless on the street because
of their meth addiction."

For gays and straights alike, meth often works its magic
through sex. At first, sex becomes so intoxicating on meth that
people can think of little else. Mary Holley, an obstetrician who
runs an antimeth ministry in Albertville, Alabama, says it's difficult for non-meth users to understand the carnal desires that

meth can fire, at least at first. Holley told the Associated Press that "the effect of an IV hit of methamphetamine is the equivalent of ten orgasms all on top of each other lasting for 30 minutes to an hour, with a feeling of arousal that lasts for another day and a half." It is only later that meth takes away the gift that it has promised. But few people realize that when they first use the drug. Under any circumstances, the sex drive can make people do foolish things. Sex on meth—gratification taken to an exponential level—can seem like heaven on earth.

It is little wonder, then, that crystal meth use is a particularly acute problem in gay bathhouses. Men frequently take a vial to a rented room, put it under a mattress, and use the drug that allows them to binge on sex with six or eight partners in a weekend. The bathhouses typically put out condoms for their customers to use. But many of the men reject them. "Some guys just throw you out of the room if you pull one out," a young gay man in a Chelsea bathhouse told the *New York Times.* "To them, rubbers are a kill-joy."

The Internet has made it possible for men who would never enter a sex club—or even admit to being gay—to "hook up" with other men and meet in private places, use drugs, and, often, engage in unsafe sex. In chat rooms, gay meth users simply type "PnP," an abbreviation for "Party and Play," to signal their willingness to take meth and have sex. At some parties organized through the Internet, a few dozen participants meet in a hotel, kick in $20 or $25 apiece to cover the tab, get high on meth, and have sex with men they have just met. The parties follow a simple routine: the men stash their clothes in plastic bags and then start using meth and having sex—often without a condom.

At some of these parties, it's easy to tell which meth users are infected with the AIDS virus—sunken cheeks, swollen neck glands, distended bellies. "If you weren't high, you'd definitely think twice about having sex with somebody who obviously has HIV," said Alex, a gay man in suburban New Jersey who has attended some of these parties. "But when you're sky-high right out of your brain, you don't care about anything in the world. You feel like nothing can be wrong, like nothing can hurt you. So you go ahead and do it and worry about it later."

Plenty of people do end up worrying about it later. In many gay neighborhoods, the number of Crystal Meth Anonymous meetings now rival the number of Alcoholics Anonymous meetings. Many of these meth users spiral deeper into their addiction after learning the devastating news that they have tested positive for the AIDS virus. Others use it as a wake-up call to get help. One of them was Peter, a forty-three-year-old New Yorker who has spent $6,000 of his own money on an ad campaign designed to scare people away from meth. He has put ads in phone booths along Eighth Avenue in New York that say, "Huge Sale, Buy Crystal, Get HIV Free." He says the ads "were meant to shock." Peter says he started using the drug at all-night dance parties. "I've tried everything in the book and never got addicted, but meth grabbed me by the throat the first time I did it," he said. "I'm a control freak. I mean, I couldn't get addicted to cigarettes. But I couldn't give crystal up." He hopes his ad campaign will make people think about the consequences before getting high on meth. "I want crystal to get the stigma that heroin has," he said.

Health departments in California and New York are now spending hundreds of thousands of dollars in a campaign to spread the word to gay men about the dangers of meth. The effort has enlisted such celebrities as John Cameron Mitchell, the director and star of the hit film *Hedwig and the Angry Itch*. Mitchell says he has seen friends waste away. "They start to look like a ghost and can't even see it," he said. "What we need are intelligent scare tactics to convince people the drug is uncool." Mayor John Duran of West Hollywood has been meeting with workers in the gay sex industry, porn filmmakers and actors, to discuss ways to combat meth use. "We didn't come through the AIDS epidemic and the battles over gays in the military and gay marriage to end up here, a community filled with drug addicts," said Duran, who is gay and HIV-positive. "We've fought too long and too hard to let this drug bring us down." The Van Ness Recovery House in Los Angeles, which specializes in drug treatment for gays and lesbians, hands out condoms with antimeth messages: "Meth Wants You for the Long Haul— It's Not Recreational Sport."

The Stop AIDS campaign in California, meanwhile, has been putting up posters in gay bars on Sunset Boulevard and Santa Monica Boulevard aimed at deglamorizing meth with ads of haggard-looking people under titles such as "Nobody Looks Their Best at 6 A.M." Jason, a leader of Stop AIDS, calls meth "the crack cocaine of the gay community." He spends hours every day visiting Internet sex sites and sending warning messages about the harm meth can cause. Antimeth crusaders remind people that the drug can take away sexual powers as quickly as it seems to grant them. If meth is used long enough, it can cause impotence. "At first, I liked taking meth because it made me tingle, and it lowered my inhibitions, so that I could be more daring," said Evan, a thirty-five-year-old gay advertising executive in the Chicago neighborhood known as Boy's Town. "It's like it tapped into some primal sexual desire. It was very hot. And I could last all night. But after a while, I needed meth to have sex at all. I couldn't get an erection if I wasn't high. Then even if I was high, it wouldn't work. By the end, I didn't even care about sex. All I cared about was getting high on meth."

Before he became a slave to meth, Jay seemed to be living life from the pages of an F. Scott Fitzgerald novel, hobnobbing with some of the hippest and most fashionable men in New York. He shared a sprawling Long Island estate with his partner, a wealthy businessman. From the outside, everything about Jay's life seemed dashing. He had more money than he could spend—"I could have shopped all day, every day"—and he socialized with men who were rich, famous, and powerful. It was a long way from his middle-class childhood in Richmond, Virginia. He thought he had it made. "I wanted people to think I had it all," he would say later. "But I was just a shell of a person."

Jay had long had a weakness for cocaine, and he could afford all he wanted. Snorting it made him feel good about himself and gave him a wonderful rush. He knew it had become a problem. In fact, he was addicted to coke, and he knew it would drag him down. Eventually, Jay found a way to kick coke: meth. He discovered it in a bathhouse on West Twentieth Street. It was during a period of deep depression. A man saw him suffering and told him he had something to cure his blues. "Here, I've got something that can help you," the man told Jay. He took a snort and never wanted to stop. "I had never experienced anything higher or more powerful," he said. "After I started with crystal, people would offer me cocaine, and I'd say, 'No thanks.' It was nothing compared to crystal." It seemed to mask all his insecurities, and it helped him convince himself he could live a lie. Though he had completed just a year of college, he inflated his résumé and told people he was highly educated. At times he believed it. "I had been a self-hating, insecure man—insecure about everything: my looks, my education, even the size of my penis," he said, "but then suddenly I was having delusions of grandeur."

Working for a high-end real estate firm in New York, Jay thought he could mix work with his newfound pleasure. He would "do a bump" and then go negotiate million-dollar deals. For a while, he got away with it. Then he started losing important documents. He missed an important closing. Soon enough, he got fired. He went from one relationship to another, none of them based on anything real or genuine. He was nothing short of a gold digger. And he needed the gold to pay for the junk—meth—he so desperately needed. He was going downhill so fast it all seemed a swirl. He lost one job after the next, and then another. He declared bankruptcy. He was evicted from his apartment. He wound up homeless, living with whoever would take him. He worked as a "call boy," turning tricks for paying customers. He took a job as a "massage therapist," which amounted to little more than masturbating other men for pay. "I sold my body and I whored my soul," he said. He grew so desperate he actually tried to become infected with HIV. He got his wish. Crazy and sick on meth, he would wander the mean streets of New York alone, an easy target for the gay bashers who beat him. He became so paranoid he heard voices in his head and talked back to them. With nowhere else to go, he slept in Dumpsters full of garbage, bugs, and rats.

Finally one morning, he decided to end the pain and misery. He stood on a ledge at a construction site, nearly four stories above the ground, and decided to jump. "I had lost faith in God," he said. "And I said to myself: If there is a God, he'll catch me—and he did catch me." Jay landed in a pile of sand that softened his fall. If he had fallen a few inches either way, he would surely have been killed. Instead, he wound up with a head held together by steel sutures. In the most dramatic, violent, and literal way, he had hit bottom. It was the best thing, he said, that ever happened to him. He entered a treatment center and got himself sober.

Jay later founded the Philadelphia Crystal Meth Task Force to spread the word about meth to the gay community. He has made posters featuring a ghastly photograph of himself in the emergency room after his crash. Next to his withered, scarred body, the copy on the poster reads: "One Bag of Crystal Meth, $60; Emergency Room Visit After Suicide Attempt, $15,000; Having Unsafe Sex While High, Free; Becoming HIV-Positive While High, Free; HIV Medication (Lifetime Supply), $200,000; Loving Yourself Enough to Stop Using Tina, Priceless."

After going through drug treatment, Jay has worked ceaselessly to bring himself down to earth. He now lives in a modest one-bedroom apartment in Philadelphia and runs a cleaning service, AngelicCleaning.com. "Cleaning other people's toilets brought me to the common denominator I needed to reach—it took away that shell of superiority and allowed me to cleanse my soul." He is grateful that he crashed. "Luckily, I lost everything, because it made me humble. It knocked the chip off my shoulder and forced me to be a man—a real man—not the scared boy that I used to be, trying to act so big and so important." He plans to spend the rest of his days helping others stay away from meth, or climb out of the gutter once meth has taken them to those depths. "The reason I talk to people about my meth addiction is that it keeps me sober," he said. "I'm scared to death of losing my sobriety. Because the next step for me is death."

CHAPTER SIX

The Young Faces of Meth

Julie held two pictures of her daughter Angela. The first was taken when the girl was twelve years old. She looked like an angel: a robust, pretty, dark-eyed girl with an innocent grin. The other picture of Angela was taken just a year later at a Des Moines juvenile detention center. It was horrifying. Angela looked as if she had been starved and beaten. She was haggard and rail-thin. Her skin looked gray. Her face was pocked with sores. Her eyes were sunken deep behind red circles.

She had run away, time and again. Things hadn't been easy at home. Her parents had divorced. They fought bitterly over custody. It surely took its toll on Angela. But there was something else going on with this girl. At times, she grew angry and withdrawn. She often seemed paranoid. She got into delinquency troubles.

At fifteen, Angela was found dead. She had shot herself in the head. Nobody can be certain what drove this former Catholic high school girl to take her life, but her mother believes she knows. "She wasn't just another screwed-up kid in the middle of a custody battle," her mother said at a press conference in Des Moines. "It was meth." Indeed, a toxicology report after Angela's death found meth in her system.

For a time, even after Angela's death, Julie didn't talk about her daughter's use of meth. She didn't think anyone would think it possible that a middle-class Iowa girl reared in good schools could succumb to this vile substance. "I never brought up meth," she said. "I just didn't believe that anyone would believe that a child that age could be involved that deeply with that drug. Today, it's everywhere. And it's so severe."

Julie has drawn on her grief to crusade against meth, taking her cause to the Iowa statehouse and speaking before other groups dedicated to stopping the spread of this poison among young people. "Those pictures are all people need to see," said Angela's mom. "I want this to be the face of meth. I want Angie to become the poster child of meth addiction."

Sadly, there are many such faces of meth these days. These are girls and boys so young they cannot go to a movie rated anything more than PG-13. But somehow they come across meth. Curiosity gets the best of them. And then the trap shuts. They cannot escape, at least not on their own, and the path is laid for the streets, or jail, or a hospital, or the morgue. Nationally, about 5 percent of high school seniors have reported using methamphetamine. In the American heartland, the numbers are much higher. A social worker in one Iowa county estimated that one-third of high school students there had tried meth.

In one Mississippi River town in 2004, police arrested a sixth grader on meth charges in the middle school. He was having severe mood swings, lashing out with anger, and showing frustration with simple tasks. An observer might have chalked it up to puberty—most people cannot imagine a sixth-grade boy being involved with meth. After the arrest, the boy pleaded guilty to the felony charge of organizing meth parties with other children. Police say he had gotten the drug from his mother's twenty-seven-year-old boyfriend. The man was charged with distributing drugs to a child. It's unclear how long the sixth grader had been using meth, but he appeared to have already become dependent on it. The judge in juvenile court wrote in the case that the boy was craving the drug several days after his arrest. She recommended inpatient treatment. The prosecuting attorney rushed the case forward because a bed had opened in a treatment center in Cedar Rapids, and the boy was transferred to the center. It was a shocking case, but he wasn't the youngest child to have used meth in the small town. An adolescent counselor at one Iowa substance abuse center said she is working with a boy who has been using meth since he was ten years old. Among the adolescents she treats for drug problems, about 70 percent have used meth. "I've seen some kids who used it and didn't even know what it was," she said. "They thought it was cocaine." But most of the teenagers she sees know exactly what they were using. "It's the trend drug right now," she said, "and they want to fit in."

Alarmed by the arrest of the sixth grader, parents packed an Iowa middle school to find out more about the drug and ways to detect its use. Many of the adults confessed that they wouldn't know what meth looked like if they found it. A police officer gave some straightforward tips. The parents were told to talk with children about all drugs. Most meth users start with cigarettes, alcohol, or marijuana before "graduating" to harder drugs. The parents were encouraged to monitor their children's cell phone records, Web site visits, and e-mail correspondence, and to feel free to look around the kids' bedrooms. "One of the resounding things I see in parents is that their kids reach the magic age of middle school, and they're suddenly 'grown up,'" the officer told the *Clinton Daily Journal.* "They're not." If parents find something suspicious, they shouldn't hesitate to call the authorities. "We do a lot of referrals for counseling," the officer said. "Our first priority is to get the kids help."

Treatment centers are starting to see more and more teenagers hooked on meth. One of them was Caroline, a lanky sixteen-year-old girl with blue eyes, curly blond hair, and braces. She liked being part of the popular crowd at her high school in a small town in Missouri. She also liked a boy named Joe, a handsome kid with a quick sense of humor and a bit of a daring streak. She thought he was the coolest. She also trusted him. So when he took her to parties where people were drinking or smoking, she figured he had it under control. Before long, she was drinking alcohol and smoking pot with him. It became a weekly ritual. But then something changed. Somebody in the group pulled out a vial one night. It looked unfamiliar. The kid said it was some great stuff. It was called meth. She tried it and felt the powerful rush. Before long, she was smoking it whenever she could. "Meth can take you places you've never been," she said later. But some were places she'd never want to go.

At one meth party, her boyfriend had to leave for a while, and he told her he'd be back later. "I felt real awkward," she said. "I begged him not to leave. But I was totally into this guy. I knew he would never let anything happen to me. I mean, I'd known him since I was thirteen. We'd spent Christmas together." He left the apartment for an hour or so. But it seemed like he was gone for an eternity. During that time, Caroline was alone with the drug dealer, and he began to look at her in a very strange way. "Joe, where are you?" she wondered to herself. Her heart was racing. The drug dealer crept nearer to Caroline, and then he touched her shoulder. "I guess he thought I owed him something," she said later, beginning to tremble, as tears spilled down her cheeks. "He like . . . forced himself onto me. He was this dirty, gross guy who smelled. I never told anybody about it." Caroline's life seemed to spin out of control. She would see things that weren't there. She imagined bugs on her skin—"meth mites," she called them—that she would desperately try to claw away, leaving bloody holes. She did things she never would have otherwise done. She did things she didn't even remember afterward. "Your morals, your principles, none of that is important when you're using meth. It changes who you are."

Michael was another Missouri teenager who stumbled into the meth quicksand. Square-jawed and muscular, he considered himself a tough boy, somebody who could handle himself in any crowd. At fifteen, he ran into a group of kids using meth and figured he'd try it himself. The first few times, he got it for free. "I got hooked right away," he said. "It took my body. It destroyed my nostrils. I couldn't blow my nose without blowing blood into the rag. It clogged up my skin and put big bumps on my face, the back of my neck." Michael injected meth with needles that a group of friends would share. It only hit him later that dirty needles could spread HIV.

Like Caroline, he became fixated with real or imagined itching while on meth. He once had a hangnail on his finger and became obsessed with trying to bite it off. He couldn't stop himself, even as the finger began to bleed profusely. He kept biting until "I had chewed off one whole side of my finger" and needed to go to the emergency room for stitches. He chewed on the inside of his mouth until it bled, and bloody spittle would run down the sides of his mouth. He got so wasted that he had a seizure, falling on a bathroom floor and flopping around as if he were being zapped by an electronic gun. But nothing could stop him from wanting more and more meth. He hid his problems from his family as long as he could, and then he stopped caring. "We'd all eat dinner together because that was important to my family," he said. "But then I just stopped coming home. Sometimes I wouldn't go home until three o'clock in the morning, and my parents would be sitting up, worried sick about me. But I couldn't even realize what was going on."

Michael crashed his senior year. He was arrested on meth-related charges and sent to prison. His parents were devastated. "When I came to the penitentiary, I could hear them crying on the phone," he said. He did a lot of crying himself. The eighteen-year-old would cover his face in the pillow and weep into the night. "I cried so hard in my bunk," he said. "I missed my family. I missed not being able to finish high school. A lot of that stuff hurts you so deep down inside in ways you didn't realize." He pines for the freedom he's lost since he entered jail. But he says he really lost his freedom the day he started using meth. "You don't have freedom when you're using this drug," he said. "The drug's got control of you."

In the 1990s, rural teenagers accounted for the vast majority of adolescents entering drug treatment facilities for meth abuse. These days, treatment centers are seeing more and more boys and girls from middle-class suburbs. For counselors who work with adolescents, treating meth users poses special challenges. "Because they're so angry, so paranoid, so obnoxious, it can be harder to get them to stay in treatment," said Mollie Greenig, a counselor at a youth addiction treatment center in Minnesota. "We're not a locked facility, and they can walk out the front door anytime they want to." Greenig says many of these adolescents have other psychological issues that also complicate their treatment. Many of the boys have been diagnosed with attention deficit disorder. Indeed, the speed-oriented effects of meth sometimes mimic—and send into high gear—the medicines that were initially prescribed for their attention problems. Greenig cited the case of one young man—an outdoorsy boy who loved to hunt and fish—who used meth because it initially helped him control his temper. "For a while, the meth allowed him to calm down and focus and get a handle on his anger issues," she said. But before long the drug would only ratchet up his temper and cloud his ability to calm down and make good decisions. It was gasoline on a burning match. Now he was not only an angry young man, but he was also hooked. On meth, he spun out of control.

Girls often turn to meth because they suffer eating disorders and see the drug as an easy way to keep their weight down. "Body image is so important to them—they see the images of skinny women in the media every day—and they see losing weight as the most important thing in their lives," said Greenig. In treatment, these girls become very worried about the weight gain that will come with recovery. Some of them have dropped up to fifty pounds. Oddly, they often don't see how terrible the meth has made them look. "When they come in, they look almost gray," said Greenig. "After they've been away from the drug for a while, the color comes back into their faces. You can see their appearances change right in front of you." In some cases, the kids also have a difficult time understanding that the drug they hoped would be a magic cure has only worsened their feelings of anxiety. One teenage boy became so frantic about his mental state that he checked himself into a psychiatric hospital. "He thought he was having a breakdown," Greenig said.

For boys and girls, the drug use almost always harms their performance in school, which only makes them hate going to class all the more. Adolescents with drug problems have often become accustomed to stealing to feed their habits and fall into criminal behavior that ranges far beyond sneaking money from a parent's purse or wallet. Some of the young people have been arrested for stealing cars, or for assault, and are sent to treatment by an order of the court. Others have grown so desperate they ask their parents for help, or the parents step in and force a child to enter a treatment program. After the drug is removed, many of these young people have other mental health problems they must address. But nothing will work until they become sober.

Some parents of meth-using children turn to therapeutic boarding schools. Some of these facilities, which are common in western states, rely on a wilderness-survival approach, using nature, and a skilled staff, to nurture self-reliance and self-respect among the troubled adolescents. Vigorous exercise is usually part of the program, as well as group therapy that requires each boy or girl to come to terms with their behavior problems. They sometimes are required to write home to parents, telling them about how they are working on their issues, as well as acknowledge how their drug use and other abusive behavior has affected others in the family. While they are in these programs, the young people are usually expected to set goals each day, and achieve them, before being advanced to a higher level with more freedom and privileges.

Counselors in some of these camps say adolescents in today's society lack the rites of passage that traditionally came with growing up—hunting for food, building shelter, caring for younger siblings—so they have turned to drugs as a way to prove to themselves that they are "growing up." These programs can run for two months or more. When the young people have completed the programs, the parents and siblings come on "reunion day," when the young people run through a nature trail to reach their families. Having been separated from their families for so long, even the most toughened, defiant teenagers will often fall weeping into the arms of Mom and Dad, brothers and sisters. Some of these programs have been hailed as lifesavers, and criticized by others as being overly punitive. One thing is certain: they are very expensive, often costing tens of thousands of dollars.

Some states have established "sober schools" for young alcohol and other drug abusers that serve as alternatives to regular high schools. These are not treatment facilities, but rather schools that allow adolescents in recovery from alcohol and other drug addictions to attend classes in a community of supportive peers where abstinence is the norm. Advocates of these schools say that sending chemically dependent kids in recovery back to regular schools is like sending a drunk back to a bar.

At regular schools, weekend parties are a fixture of the social scene, and that can mean a dangerous landscape for young people trying to stay away from drugs and alcohol. At Sobriety High in Minnesota, students are required to go to Twelve Step meetings on their own time. They also meet in "group" as a required class and earn a grade for it. In these sessions, they discuss their struggles and progress in staying clean, often writing assignments about specific steps they will take that very day to help in recovery. If a student relapses at Sobriety High and acknowledges it to the staff, chances are good the teenager will get a second chance. If he continues to use drugs or drink, he will be kicked out. Sobriety High, a charter school, has three campuses. Each school keeps the enrollment small, about forty-five or fifty kids. Students can choose to come to these schools. In some cases, the court has ordered them to attend. The schools have been so popular they have a waiting list.

For adolescents who have been using for years, it can be

difficult to imagine a life without alcohol or other drugs, said Judy Hanson, the director at Sobriety High. "They learn that it isn't going to be boring to be sober, which is what they're fearing," she said. "But we've got a wide range of very interesting students. We've got athletes. We've got musicians. These kids are fun. They're hip. This isn't a boring place." Besides classes, the students have extracurricular activities like intramural sports, boating, hiking, cooking, a winter formal dance, a student council. Each day, the students keep a log of their activities, which includes goals to be accomplished by the end of the afternoon.

Not surprisingly, plenty of young people are not happy when they arrive. "We tell them, 'Give it a month—give it two weeks,'" said Hanson. They also tell the adolescents they must be willing to make a break from their old lives. "Are you willing to get rid of your old friends?" they are asked. "Because you must tell them you're not going to be able to be around them." Breaks at Sobriety High "can be scary times," Hanson said, because the young people go home and risk facing situations that will tempt them to use. If a student starts using a substance again, it's most often the other students who detect it first. They come to care deeply about one another. And they are quick to notice signs of drug trouble in a classmate. "It's hard to con a con," said Hanson.

A pretty teenager named Jenn knows how it works. When Jenn was in the eighth grade in suburban Minneapolis, she seemed to have the world by the tail. The daughter of a business executive—her dad was a senior vice president for an international finance company—Jenn lived in a beautiful two-story house with a cool recreation room in the basement. She wore hip clothes and kept a collection of the best music. The boys were wowed by her good looks: long black hair and pierc-

Eroding the Mind

Researchers have mapped brain decay caused by methamphetamine use. The damage affected memory, emotion and reward systems.

Average difference in brain tissue volume of methamphetamine users, as compared with non-users:

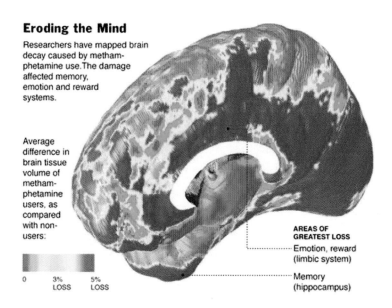

0   3% LOSS   5% LOSS

AREAS OF GREATEST LOSS

.... Emotion, reward (limbic system)

.... Memory (hippocampus)

Courtesy of Paul Thompson, Kiralee Hayashi, Arthur Toga, and Edythe London/UCLA

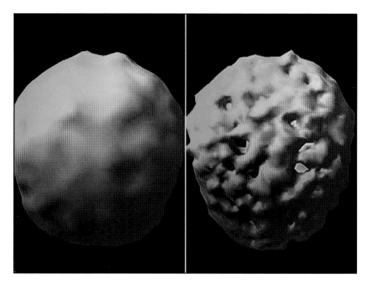

SPECT imaging measures a brain's cerebral blood flow and activity patterns. Compare a SPECT image of a healthy brain (left) with that of a twenty-eight-year-old meth addict with eight years of heavy use (right).
Courtesy of Amen Clinics, Inc.

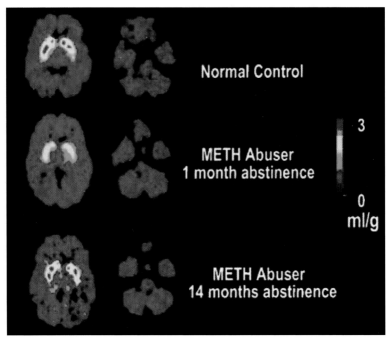

A brain scan shows improved brain function after fourteen months without methamphetamine. ©2005 by the Society for Neuroscience

Meth varies in color, depending on the ingredients used and the processing time.
Photo by Ron Hoeschen (Banta Corporation)

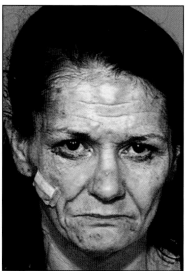

Before and after pictures reveal the damaging physical effects after three-and-a-half years of meth use.
Courtesy of Multnomah County (Oregon) Sheriff's Office

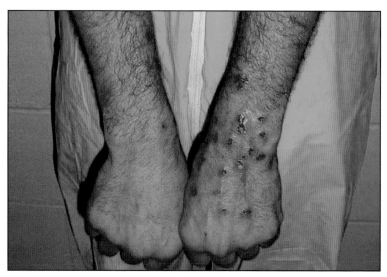

Meth users repeatedly scratch at imaginary bugs, creating open sores called "crank bugs."
Courtesy of North Metro Task Force, Adams County, Colorado

Homes that harbor clandestine meth labs are most often filthy and disheveled (top). Burn marks cover a stove top used to cook meth (bottom).
Courtesy of Chisago County (Minnesota) Sheriff's Office

In homes meth and the ingredients used to make it are easily accessible to all family members. A container with a chemical sits open in the refrigerator near the milk and apple juice (top); toys lie next to a dirty ashtray and a foil with meth (bottom).
Courtesy of Chisago County (Minnesota) Sheriff's Office

Meth labs are increasingly being discovered in residential areas.
Courtesy of Chisago County (Minnesota) Sheriff's Office

Empty packets of medicine that contains ephedrine or pseudoephedrine, an essential ingredient used to make meth, are discovered in a kitchen.
Courtesy of Chisago County (Minnesota) Sheriff's Office

To begin the cleanup process, trained agents first remove and separate all the toxic ingredients from the lab (top). Direct exposure to the chemicals can be deadly, so agents are careful to work in sealed suits that must be washed down afterward (bottom).

Courtesy of Chisago County (Minnesota) Sheriff's Office

Meth lab sites either go through a costly cleanup or are condemned (top).
A poem expresses the agony of a meth addict (bottom).
Courtesy of Chisago County (Minnesota) Sheriff's Office

ing blue eyes. On top of everything else, she was a star swimmer. She had been competing in club swimming since she was eight years old, and people were astonished by her fast times in the 200-yard medley and 100-yard backstroke.

Jenn was a popular girl with plenty of friends. During a snow day, she and a group of boys and girls went to hang out at a friend's house. The friend's parents were at work, so the teenagers were free of supervision for the day. As they talked and giggled, one of the kids pulled something out of his pocket. It was marijuana. She decided to go ahead and try it. "I liked it," she said. "I liked it a lot." She smoked pot a few more times that year, but seemed to be keeping everything together. When she started her freshman year, she was moved up to the varsity swimming team, a huge accomplishment in her big, competitive school. She was going gangbusters, swimming like a champ. Everybody figured she was headed for a college scholarship. She vowed to stay straight during swim season, and she did. But when the season was over, she found herself with a lot of spare time.

At a friend's house, during a sleepover, some boys sneaked beer into the basement. It was just enough for the boys, so Jenn and her friend went upstairs and poked around in the parents' liquor cabinet. They found a gallon bottle of Canadian Windsor and took it downstairs. That night, Jenn drank fourteen shots of whiskey. She remembers coming in and out and throwing up. She blacked out and woke up in the morning. She was tired and hungover. Though she felt sick from the alcohol, she knew it was something she wanted to try again. By the end of her freshman year, she was smoking pot three or four times a week and drinking whenever she got the chance.

Early in Jenn's sophomore year, her mother "overheard me talking on the telephone about smoking weed." Her mom confronted her, and Jenn promised that she would never do it again. But she didn't keep her promise. Her grades started to slip, and her swimming coach got wind of the talk that she was smoking marijuana. Before the season, the coach told her that she'd be suspended for a few meets, but that she could practice with the team. If she stayed straight, she could start participating in the meets in a few weeks. She made her way eventually back into competition. But during one of the meets, she did something that showed her judgment wasn't working properly. She and another girl went outside the school and smoked a cigarette. The coach spotted her and immediately kicked her off the team.

By this time, Jenn was also abusing prescription drugs she was given by kids being treated for attention deficit disorder. The meds speeded her up, made her talk a mile a minute, and kept her up for long periods of time. Her parents decided something had to be done. They put her in a residential treatment program and later enrolled her at Sobriety High. The sobriety wouldn't last.

During her stint in treatment, she had met a girl from Wisconsin who had an addiction to meth. The two became pals, and after they left the facility, they made plans to get together. When Jenn went to visit her friend's home, the girls took a walk in the woods, and her friend gave her a "gift." It was a gram of meth—the very substance that the friend had admitted had "ruined her life." Jenn smoked it—and loved it. "It's like nothing I'd ever tried before," she said. "It was so cool. It made me feel powerful. It made you feel like you were in control. It wasn't like pot or 'shrooms, where you're seeing things that aren't there. I felt like meth just made you better, smarter, stronger. It made me feel like I was best friends with everybody."

She brought some of the meth home to Minnesota and told

her boyfriend about it. He'd used meth before, too. Now the two of them were using it together. They would smoke it every chance they could. She hid the meth in a mint tin she kept in her purse and never let it far from her sight. She fooled her parents into believing that she was straight, at least for a while.

But the other students at Sobriety High knew she was using drugs. During the school's group session, with forty-two of the boys and girls gathered to talk about the issues of addiction and recovery, one of them delivered the news out loud. "Jenn is using meth," the kid told the others. Jenn gasped. The other students turned and looked at her. "I was so scared," she said. "And I was angry." But she wasn't entirely surprised. "I know I can tell what other kids are using, and they could tell about me." She had been skipping classes and generally acting crabby, she said, signs that can be a giveaway that a student isn't staying sober. The next day, she was met at the front door of the school by the program director, Judy, who delivered an edict. "You can't be here," the director told Jenn. "You've got to have someone come and pick you up." She called a cousin, who drove her to her aunt's home and later called her parents. Her mom and dad were angry and upset. But she vowed to them that she was going to stay sober. It was a one-day suspension. She returned to school, and then two weeks later Sobriety High recessed for winter break. Her vow to stay sober went out the window. "I was using meth, alcohol, and weed almost every day," she said. "But meth was the one I really wanted."

Her parents could tell that she was in trouble. They confronted her. By this time, Jenn was so deep into meth that she couldn't think straight. She met her parents with a tone of defiance. "I told them I don't want to be sober anymore," she said. "I'm not going to give it up." She was staying out at all hours, sometimes spending the night at her boyfriend's, who had been kicked out of his own home and was living with someone else. "Christmas was weird," she said. "We were all together as a family, but that night I left and went out with my boyfriend and got high again."

The day before New Year's Eve, she got into a fight with her boyfriend, and he kicked her out. Cracked on meth, she wandered alone, feeling as if she might freeze to death. She was also hallucinating—seeing things that weren't there, thinking that people were chasing her. Feeling panicked, she went to a pay phone and called 911. "I was delirious and strung out," she said. "I called the police dispatcher and told them I was cold." Minnesota was in a deep freeze, and Jenn wasn't even wearing a coat. The dispatcher looked at the clock. It was 4 A.M. "Why are you out so late?" the dispatcher asked her. "What are you doing?" Jenn simply repeated, over and over, "I'm cold." The owner of the gas station where Jenn made the call saw her and called the police. Moments later, three squad cars and an ambulance arrived. One of the officers said he'd take charge. He took Jenn into his car and drove her home. Her parents had been up all night frantic with worry about her. The police officer told them that it appeared that Jenn had overdosed on something. "Your daughter needs go to the hospital," he told them. Her parents took her to the emergency room right away.

"The next thing I remember was being in a hospital bed with an IV in each arm," Jenn said. "There were some sticky things on my chest. I was on a heart monitor." Her parents sat near her in the hospital room. It seemed the room was heavy with worry and heartbreak. The next morning, Jenn was released from the hospital. But that night, New Year's Eve, she skipped out again. She went to a casino with some friends. They drank and used drugs. Sometime that night, her cell phone rang. It was an older brother, trying to track her down. "I'm coming to pick you up." Her brother and two other young men scooped her up from the casino, then drove to the drug dealer's house to find Jenn's boyfriend. They were outraged that he had kicked her out, leaving her stoned on drugs in the cold. They found the young man and beat him severely. Jenn didn't try to stop the beating. It was just one of the many ugly consequences of her drug taking that Jenn still regrets.

Jenn's brother took her home. She spent the next few days drinking and getting high. But even she could no longer deny that her world had spun out of control. She couldn't take this kind of life anymore. Her weight had dropped from 125 pounds to 92 pounds. During one period, she had gone without sleep for ten days. Her hair was greasy because she had stopped bathing herself regularly. There were cold sores and cracked skin around her lips from the meth use. Finally she went to her dad and broke down. "I'm desperate," she told him, "I need help."

Jenn's dad had a profound level of understanding. He had quit drinking nine years ago. He knew that problems with alcohol and other drugs were more than just a matter of willpower. He also knew that relapse was part of recovery. Her parents made some calls, and within days Jenn was enrolled in another treatment facility. After graduating from the treatment center, Jenn went to live in a halfway house with sixteen other girls, all of them under age eighteen. "Most of us were meth abusers," she said. "We talked about life, about how things had gone in our past, and how drugs had taken control of us." The halfway house was a big Victorian home in a suburb of Minneapolis. At the halfway house, Jenn learned how to live with other girls as part of a family. She learned to cook and clean and do laundry, tasks that she'd never had to worry about before. "I learned to make spaghetti and sloppy joes," she said. When her parents would come for a visit, it was very emotional. "They were very proud of me," she said. Her family met with a therapist and talked about honing the skills they needed to get along better. Jenn and her mom had always butted heads, even before drugs became a problem. "We were so much alike," Jenn said, "that was part of the problem."

After leaving the halfway house, Jenn enrolled in another alternative school for three months. At the end of the year, she was told she could return to Sobriety High. She now works three days a week at her uncle's sunglasses shop. She attends Alcoholics Anonymous meetings three times a week, where she's far from the youngest person. One of them is just fourteen. Jenn has also cultivated a spiritual life. She grew up Catholic, and although she doesn't go to church anymore, she prays every day for her sobriety. "I pray to a God of my understanding," she said, describing her Higher Power as "something more important than me." She also has a boyfriend, a young man in his second year of college who also attends AA meetings. He hopes to be a psychiatrist. At Sobriety High, Jenn has kept her grades high, about 3.6 on a four-point scale. Since treatment, she hasn't earned a grade less than a B and plans to enroll at a Catholic nursing college in Minnesota. She wants to work with young children. She no longer craves meth or any other drug. "I have no desire to drink or get high anymore," she said. "Praying has helped me remove that obsession." She does some public speaking at schools, churches, and the Kiwanis Club. "At the rate I was going, I'd either be dead or prostituting myself," she said. "Getting sober saved my life."

CHAPTER SEVEN

The Battle against Meth

"Smurfing," the meth addicts call it: driving from one store to the next to buy packages of cold medicines and other meth-making supplies. In the shopping spree, they might hit dozens of towns and even cross state lines. The goal is to buy hundreds or thousands of tablets of cold medicine containing pseudo-ephedrine or ephedrine without arousing the suspicion of store clerks who might alert police. The pills are the vital ingredient for people who "cook" meth. Sometimes addicts hire them-selves out as smurfs, trading the cold pills for the finished prod-uct. In other cases, it's the cooks themselves who do the smurfing. One of these cooks was an Oklahoman named Ricky Ray Malone. Early one morning, Malone was brewing a batch of the drug, just as police say he'd done so many times before. This time, he didn't even bother to hide. Or maybe he didn't know quite where he was. He was pretty cooked himself. Whatever his thinking, Ricky Ray Malone was making meth right out on the Oklahoma roadside, plain as daylight. It was as if it were the Fourth of July and Ricky Ray was just grilling some steaks. No big deal. But it wasn't Independence Day. It was the morning after Christmas, and Malone was cooking the poison in the trunk of a Geo Spectrum parked at the side of a country road.

A motorist noticed the spectacle—no longer such an odd sight in Oklahoma—and alerted the police. It was not yet dawn when State Trooper Nikky Joe Green took the call about the suspicious activity. The day before, Green, thirty-five, had celebrated Christmas with his wife, Linda, and their three young daughters. Now it was time for the little ones to play with their new toys and for the grown-ups to get back to work. On a frozen, dreary morning, Green made the short drive down to the roadside to investigate the complaint. He would never make it home. When the officer arrived, he saw Malone and the meth lab. He confronted the thirty-year-old and put him under arrest. But when he tried to handcuff the meth cook, the officer lost control of his revolver. The men wrestled, and Malone was able to grab the gun. He forced the trooper to the ground. On this lonely country road, at the mercy of a drug addict, Green begged for his life, a scene that was captured by a video recorder installed on the dash of the squad car.

"Please, don't kill me!" Green pleaded. "I've got kids and a wife." Then he spoke once more, in what seems a prayer. "Lord—Jesus Christ." These were his last words. Malone pointed at Green's head and pulled the trigger.

A Comanche County jury in May 2005 sentenced Malone to death for the murder of Green. The verdict surprised no one, not even Malone's lawyer, who had hoped that the killer's drug-induced craziness, and the fact that he'd been awake for twenty days, would be considered. Malone testified that he was having hallucinations that a robber was attacking him, and that he was in a fight for his life. His lawyer could scarcely negate the horror that jurors watched on the video. She said to the jurors plaintively that this is what meth can do to a person.

Malone now sits on death row, a condemned murderer and one of the most vilified figures in Oklahoma. It is difficult now to recall Malone as a man and not a monster. But like his victim, Malone was himself once a public servant. He was a fire-fighter and an emergency medical technician. A native of Oklahoma, he had dedicated himself to rescuing the sick and injured and saving lives, not destroying them. But that was before meth swallowed him whole. No profession is immune to crystal. Health workers, teachers, police officers—people leading the battle against drugs—have succumbed to meth. In the little Kentucky town of Sebree, authorities say it even snared the respected chief of police, Bobby Sauls, known as a kindly middle-aged man with snow-white hair who was a devout member of the General Baptist Church.

With other illicit drugs, such as heroin and cocaine, law enforcement agencies go after the big-time dealers to try to choke off the supply. This isn't always possible with meth, where the "supplier" is often the local store and the ingredients to make it are legal and easy to find. But that's exactly what Oklahoma lawmakers targeted in the state's battle against meth: the stores. In 2004, Oklahoma enacted the nation's most restrictive law for obtaining cold and allergy remedies that contain ephedrine or pseudoephedrine. There are many ways to make meth. But all of them require ephedrine or pseudoephedrine. Without that active ingredient, it's impossible to make the drug. The new law classifies medicines such as Sudafed, Claritin-D, Tylenol Flu products, and hundreds of others as Schedule V drugs. Controlled substances are classified on a range of one to five, with five being the least dangerous. But the classification means cold and allergy medicines must be kept behind the counter of a pharmacy or in a secured case. Moreover, the buyer of the medicine must show photo identification and sign a written log or receipt relating to the sale. This process makes it possible to keep a record of who is buying the medicine.

The measure restricts the amount of pseudoephedrine that can be purchased to nine grams within a thirty-day period, except with a prescription from a physician. Liquid-filled capsules and gel capsules are exempted from the measure because, while they can be used to make meth, the yield is extremely low and usually not worth the effort. Under the law, simply possessing a sufficient amount of materials other than pseudoephedrine or ephedrine needed to make meth can constitute "intent" to make or sell the drug, which makes it easier for police and prosecutors to build their cases. The law also allows judges to deny bond to people who have been arrested for making meth or to those who appear to be addicted to it. The new law was named after Trooper Green, as well as two other Oklahoma law enforcement officers killed in the battle against meth: David "Rocky" Eales, who was shot to death while busting a meth lab, and Matt Evans, who was killed in a high-speed chase of a man high on meth.

Drug cops on the street say restricting the "precursors"—the elements used to make meth—is much more effective than trying to chase down every drug user. "It's absurd to think we're going to make even a dent in meth by busting them," said one undercover narcotics officer. "There's way too many of them. And it takes too long to bust them. I'm afraid there's only one thing that's going to make meth go away—when something better comes along to replace it." Arrests for meth-related cases in Oklahoma jumped tenfold between 1994 and 2003. Prosecutors in the state are known for being tough. But the meth cases began to overrun the resources of the prosecutors' offices to try them and the capacity of the state's prison system to hold them. The backlog grew so heavy that police in some counties complained that most cases were being dismissed or reduced. It just wasn't possible to lock them all up. To help with the burgeoning inmate population, the state legislature gave the prison system an extra $20 million. But the overcrowding was so great that it led to a huge jump in prisoners being given parole—a nearly 500 percent increase between 1997 and 2002. Even that didn't leave enough room for the next wave of Oklahomans convicted of drug crimes. "It didn't matter if we took them off the street and put them in jail," said Nancy Pellow, an analyst with the state legislature. "Chances are they'd be out soon and go back to making meth. And when you took one away, ten more would step in to take their place." So Oklahoma began the movement to treat cold medicines like the serious drugs they can become when cooked. In doing that, the state was taking business away from some stores, like convenience shops, and demanding that pharmacies step up and play a bigger role in making sure the medicine didn't fall into the wrong hands.

Many retail groups have howled in protest. The National Association of Chain Drug Stores released a statement complaining that the measure would force highly trained pharmacists to take on a duty more fitting for nightclub bouncers: "Doctors of pharmacy are too valuable to be relegated the status of cold medicine gatekeepers, a duty that requires barely more training or knowledge than clerks who sell cigarettes or alcohol." Organizations speaking for convenience stores, meanwhile, pointed to the frightening specter of rural children—those whose families might live a long distance from pharmacies— becoming sick in the middle of the night with nowhere for their parents to buy medicine.

But advocates of the new law say it was the diminishing profits, not the sick children, that most concerned the convenience stores—and for good reason. The Oklahoma legislature pointed to findings that many of these stores were making more money on cold medicine than on Coca-Cola products. The license of a filling station and convenience store operator in Arizona was recently revoked after records showed that he sold more cold medicine than gasoline. In some cases, the pseudo-ephedrine was being sold in such bulk orders that pickup trucks would back up to the rear door of the store. In other stores, shoplifters would come into a store just before closing and brazenly steal as many packages as they could hold, then run off into the darkness.

Not all retailers balked at the efforts to restrict the sale of cold medicines. Target, Wal-Mart, and Albertsons pulled the medicines from the shelves and placed them behind the counter. Financial analysts say some of the big stores had started to worry about incurring major lawsuits if the remedies they sold were found to be used in criminal activities. The Oklahoma measure is showing promise at reducing the number of meth-making incidents. In some counties, arrests for the manufacture of meth has dropped by 70 to 80 percent, according to Mark Woodward, a spokesman for the Oklahoma Bureau of Narcotics. "We would have been thrilled with a 10 to 20 percent drop—we didn't expect anything like this," he said. "We've now got task forces that have not worked a meth lab in months. That means they're being freed up to actually go work on other drug cases. There's a lot of investigative work that can be accomplished when you don't need to have a guy spend four hours inspecting a mason jar and a Crock-Pot in some lab."

Legal experts caution that it's too early to judge the ultimate degree of success of the Oklahoma measure. But legislatures in other states have rushed to model the Oklahoma law. Similar measures have already been approved in Iowa, Oregon, Tennessee, Kentucky, Arkansas, Kansas, West Virginia, Wyoming, North Dakota, Florida, Mississippi, Alabama, and Washington. Another twenty or so states are considering such measures. On the national level, Senator Dianne Feinstein of California has called for a federal bill that would replicate many features of the Oklahoma law, especially the requirement that cold remedies be sold only by licensed pharmacies.

The restrictive measures on pseudoephedrine and ephedrine have annoyed some consumers. They resent the inconvenience of going through a pharmacy for cold tablets they could once purchase while filling up the SUV with gasoline. The drugstore lobby, meanwhile, says the measures will prove futile as long as Americans want to get high. "So long as people are addicted to drugs," the drugstore lobby declared in a statement, "they will find ways to get them." Rather than restrict the sale of these medicines, the drugstore group has urged that stores simply pay closer attention to the customers. The group touted the Meth Watch project, which trains clerks in stores to look for the familiar signs of "smurfs" who appear to be buying supplies to make meth and then to report the activity to the police. Some of these cooks are more obvious than others.

At a Kmart in a small midwestern town, a man made purchases of camper fuel and other items, then strolled to the pharmacy area to buy cold medicine. The man soon disappeared into the restroom for what seemed a very long time. When it came time to close the store, a clerk went into the restroom to alert the man and found he was operating a meth lab in a stall. Police were summoned and the man was arrested in the Kmart washroom. The discount store chain believes that educating clerks about the buying patterns of meth producers can stop its production without penalizing law-abiding customers. The group also believes federal drug enforcement agencies should be spending more money to catch drug peddlers and users. The group noted that the Drug Enforcement Administration spends $700 million a year on eradicating coca plants in South America, but only $140 million on tracking and investigating the flow of pseudoephedrine and ephedrine. Pfizer Inc., the maker of Sudafed, once opposed the measures to restrict the sale of pseudoephedrine and ephedrine. But the company reversed its position after releasing its new Sudafed PE, a nasal decongestant that does not contain the drug. Antimeth forces hailed the turnaround of the giant drug maker, but chastised it for taking so long.

Besides passing new restrictions on cold tablets, some states are also moving to more carefully secure anhydrous ammonia, the crop fertilizer that is often a key to making meth. In most of the Corn Belt, the big white anhydrous ammonia tanks have long been part of the country landscape. Motorists from the city often see these tanks being pulled along country roads by a tractor, usually without a clue about what's inside. The tanks contain the nitrogen mix that has helped boost American crop production in contemporary times to levels never known back in the days when cow manure was the standard fertilizer. Cooks covet anhydrous ammonia for its power to make some of the strongest and purest meth found anywhere. That's why so many midwestern farmers in recent years have woken early and gone out to find their anhydrous ammonia tanks have vanished. In one case in Kansas, some eighty-two tons of anhydrous ammonia went missing from a farmer's co-op. It takes only a few dozen gallons to make a big batch of meth. But this was enough anhydrous ammonia to fill five semi-tractor trailer trucks.

Theft of anhydrous ammonia—or anything else—was not something farmers of earlier generations worried about much.

Now the state of Iowa is handing out free locks to farmers in some counties and asking them to secure their tanks to protect against meth-cooking thieves. A survey of the counties using the locks saw a slight decrease in meth-lab seizures. The counties without the lock program, meanwhile, saw a jump of 112 percent in such labs, said Marvin Van Haaften, the state's drug czar. Virtually all of the farmers have been willing to cooperate, he told reporters, except for a few "grumpy old guys" who didn't want to change their ways.

Agricultural scientists are also devising ways to take anhydrous ammonia out of meth production. One company is marketing a solution that dyes the colorless gas a pinkish hue. If thieves steal the fertilizer, the dye leaves stains on their skin and clothes, as well as on the ground around the tanks. The color signals to farmers that their tanks have been disturbed by intruders. It also helps law enforcement authorities track down the pink-stained meth cooks. Even the meth made from such anhydrous ammonia will have the stain.

Researchers are also working to find a way that anhydrous ammonia would be rendered useless in the making of meth. The theory is that adding calcium nitrate to ammonia will react competitively with lithium, a key ingredient in meth making. Removing anhydrous ammonia from the meth mix would stifle production of the drug, researchers believe, and guard against the violent reaction the fertilizer triggers. Anhydrous ammonia, which is stored under high pressure as a liquid, turns to a freezing gas with a temperature of minus 28 degrees Fahrenheit when released. It is so strong it can burn the skin, throat, and lungs, and it can even cause blindness. When thieves steal anhydrous ammonia from a tank, they sometimes leave a valve open, which can poison anybody who breathes the air. A theft at a fertilizer plant in Pleasant Plain, Ohio, released a burning cloud of the chemical—a thick, gray cloud that was floating about two feet off the ground when firefighters arrived. Some 280 residents were rousted from their beds in the middle of the night and told they had to evacuate. A firefighter found an open valve and closed it. In most farm states, authorities say there is a break-in at an anhydrous ammonia tank virtually every night.

Besides clamping down on meth precursors, police and prosecutors are trying to track the trail of the drug by "working backward"—looking for meth connections in certain types of crimes, especially identity theft. Many crime experts say the rise in identity theft is directly connected to the soaring number of meth addicts. Senator Maria Cantwell of Washington State has called on the U.S. Department of Justice to study the connection between identity theft and meth addiction. Spokane County Sheriff Mark Stern said that nearly every case of ID theft in his jurisdiction was tied to methamphetamine. The thieves typically ransack mailboxes at night, usually working on those close to the road. They're looking for checks, almost always in a search for money to feed a drug habit. When they find a check, the thieves use a chemical solution to wash off most of the printing, but keep the signature. They change the payee to cash. They can also cash checks by forging driver's licenses, a crime that has become relatively easy with a laptop, a printer, and a lamination machine.

Detectives who bust meth labs say it has become common to find mountains of stolen mail in these homes. The effects of the drug seem to fit the crime ideally: meth addicts stay awake and focused for days on end, leaving them with plenty of time and energy to steal from mailboxes and cars and to hack into computer accounts. Moreover, meth typically has an obsessive-compulsive effect on the psychology of the user. That makes people high on meth ideally suited for mind-numbing tasks like piecing together bits of shredded documents. These "skills" are well known to the organized crime elements that specialize in identity theft. Police say the ringleaders will trade "meth for mail," providing addicts with an endless supply of the drug as long as they produce plenty of stolen information.

Identity theft is a trade that meth addicts often teach one another during the days-long bingeing. Detectives say addicts will often bring computers to meth parties, as they make fraudulent documents or spend the night trying to hack into personal accounts online. Noting that identity theft has grown at the same time that meth use has skyrocketed, Senator Cantwell has asked the Department of Justice to study whether there is a correlation. Most detectives already suspect there is a strong tie. If so, federal money and legal power can be used to attack meth, since identity theft almost always crosses state lines and therefore becomes a federal offense.

Police are also looking closely for meth connections in other crimes, such as car theft, sexual abuse, and domestic battery. Meth cooks often "borrow" a car for purposes of cooking the drug in the backseat or trunk and then ditch the car when they're done. Sexual abuse of children, especially in homes where a woman's drug-using boyfriend spends time around her children, is usually a clear signal that meth is a likely culprit. Domestic violence, too, has surged in places where meth is abundant. It is a scene that has become familiar to authorities from farm towns on the Great Plains to gay advocates in the East Village of New York: angry, paranoid meth addicts becoming violent with a partner, usually because they believe they are cheating with someone else. A few years ago, police happened upon these cases and chalked them up to run-of-the-mill domestic cases. Now they're looking for evidence of meth, especially if the people—the assailant or the victim—show signs of paranoia.

No matter how they attack the problems of meth, law enforcement officials acknowledge they are waging a difficult battle. Even if restricting meth precursors such as cold tablets proves successful in reducing the number of makeshift labs, the demand for the drug is going to be hard to quell, especially since so many people have now developed addictions. Indeed, some drug task forces in rural areas say the organized drug cartels have already stepped into the void created by any reduction in home-based labs. These dealers working for the "super labs" peddle a form of meth called "ice" that is more pure and powerful than the variety cooked by amateurs. One federal drug investigator put it this way: "Ice is to meth what crack is to cocaine." While the homemade meth might have a purity of 30 percent, the drug made in organized Mexican labs is more likely to be 80 or 90 percent pure, and that much more powerful.

Some of these labs have been busted in California and Washington State, where detectives have found people in possession of literally hundreds of thousands of cold pills. Some of the pills are bought illicitly overseas, sometimes in the Middle East. Investigators believe there might be a link to these drug profits and money used for terrorist activities, though no solid connection has yet been made. Some of the cold pills are smuggled from Canada, as well, with big tractor-trailer trucks driving the pseudoephedrine from Windsor across the border to Detroit and then veering off to supply addicts in the western United States. Arrests at big meth-making labs on the Mexican and Canadian borders have tripled in the last few years. Unlike freelance meth cooks, who usually make the drug to feed their own habits, organized dealers tend to be smarter and more ruthless in the way they do business. These are illicit businesspeople who rarely use the drug themselves, but rather see addicts as an easy way to make big money.

In Kentucky, the Drug Enforcement Administration recently issued a bulletin warning that these sophisticated dealers are now vigorously meeting the demands of meth addicts unable to find the cold tablets they need to make their own meth. According to the DEA notice: "Mexican organizations first infiltrate the market by offering high quality methamphetamine at low prices, amassing a large customer base that comes to prefer the superior product over the locally produced 'hillbilly meth.' Once the customer base is firmly established, they raise prices." Such a scheme, the drug agency warned, is "currently under way" in much of rural America. There is no question there is a ready market of addicts. To these meth-starved people, it won't much matter where the drug starts its journey, as long as it eventually gets to them.

CHAPTER EIGHT

Bursting at the Seams:
Drug Users behind Bars

In the tall corn country of Indiana, Vigo County is a classic outpost on the midwestern prairie. People take pride in its down-to-earth culture and solid Hoosier values: hard work, good schools, and strong churches. It has never been the most exciting place. But people in small-town Indiana don't go much for flash and dazzle. They prefer the quieter pleasures and comforts. Little League ball games. Fourth of July fireworks. It means something to be able to wave hello to the passing car on a drive down a country road and to get a wave in return, even if you don't know who is behind the wheel. It's about neighborliness and trust. As people in these parts like to say, it's the ideal place to raise kids. One of the best things about life in Vigo County has always been the feeling of safety. Plenty of people go to bed at night without locking the door. Some people don't even own a set of house keys.

For many years, the old jailhouse in Terre Haute, the county seat, had plenty of vacancies. There just weren't that many criminals to house. But then something changed. The jail was getting full, so full it became overcrowded on some nights. Three years ago, the county bit the bullet, despite its strapped budget, and financed a major expansion of the facility. They doubled its capacity. Officials figured that would take care of its inmate needs for a very long time. Within three months, the jail was filled again. The increase seemed astonishing. So the county's new sheriff, Jon Marvel, did some research on exactly who was occupying all these bunks. It turned out that a staggering 85 percent of the inmates were in jail on methamphetamine charges. The overcrowding has only gotten worse. Mattresses are spread out on floors, with prisoners stuffed together, cheek to jowl. The capacity of the new jail is 268. But on one recent weekend, 305 inmates were housed there.

"There hasn't been a week in the last three years that we haven't been over the limit," Sheriff Marvel said. He said the overcrowding amounts to a tinderbox of danger. "When you've got people sleeping on the floor at night, somebody's going to need to get up and go to the restroom, and they'll step on somebody else," he said. "These are people that are not in the best mood anyway. So now you've got pushing and jostling. Fights break out. We end up sending people to the hospital for broken jaws, stitches to the forehead."

The overcrowded jail condition in Vigo County is a microcosm of the nation's penal system. Jails and prisons across the country have become overwhelmed with drug offenders. More than any other drug, meth is by far the chief reason that jails are bursting at the seams in rural regions. It is putting a severe financial crunch on the coffers of these counties. "The minute these guys walk into our doors, the taxpayers are responsible for them," said Marvel, "and the costs are becoming astronomical."

In 1999, the budget to operate the jail in Vigo County was $812,000. In 2005, it is nearly $3 million, and climbing.

Even before meth became such a scourge in the American heartland, the nation's prisons were becoming overwhelmed with drug offenders. The move to incarcerate more drug offenders dates at least to the Rockefeller drug laws in New York State in the 1960s. But the movement to incarcerate drug users accelerated nationwide in 1982, when the Reagan Administration declared the War on Drugs. In state after state, penalties for drug use have become more severe. In most states, sentences for meth offenders average terms of more than six years, and many states are now considering measures to make the punishments even more severe.

The political calculus of the drug laws is simple. Many Americans are profoundly frightened by the dangers of drugs, especially a substance as wicked as meth, and demand that drastic measures be taken to remedy the problem. A majority of politicians, keenly aware of this climate, virtually race one another to pass stiffer penalties and lock up more offenders. And for sensible reasons: it can be political suicide to appear to be soft on drugs. In the age of sound bites and attack ads, any candidate who demurs on the lock-'em-up strategy for drug offenders risks being portrayed as a bleeding-heart wimp. Talking tough, and voting that way, is the wiser political course. One Texas lawmaker who called for a rather severe form of punishment a few years ago—cutting off the hands of drug dealers—surely raised some eyebrows. But he also won the election.

As of 2005, America imprisons 2.1 million people, a record number, and one that will almost surely continue to soar in coming years. In 1985, the national incarceration rate was 313 per 100,000; today it is 715 per 100,000. The nation jails more people than does all of Europe combined, despite the nation having 100 million fewer people. The driving force behind the increase is the stricter penalties for drug offenders. The United States now jails nearly as many people for drug offenses as it did for all crimes twenty-five years ago. The percentage of women in jails is climbing at about twice the men's rate. According to the Bureau of Prisons, some 80 percent of women in prison are being held for drug offenses. In places where meth use has become a crisis, the growth in inmates is most explosive. In Arkansas, the number of women in state penitentiaries has grown a staggering 72 percent since 1995, while the growth among male inmates in the state has been a mere whopping 47 percent. In Minnesota, the number of inmates serving time in penitentiaries for meth has jumped 628 percent between 2001 and 2004. When it comes to talking tough, the nation is putting its money where its mouth is. Spending for prisons has been the fastest-growing part of the budget in most states. That money has to come from somewhere. Between 1985 and 2000, states spent six times more for prisons than for schools.

As politically popular as locking up drug addicts might be, the big question looms: Does it work? Studies show that two-thirds of offenders are arrested for new crimes within three years of being released. Some 80 percent of people in jails and prisons have alcohol or other drug problems, according to Barbara Tombs, the president of the National Sentencing Guidelines Commission, which studies justice policies. "If they don't get proper treatment, they're going to come out with the same problems they went in with," said Tombs. "Prisons often are not equipped to provide the treatment that's needed." In some states, only about 1 percent of the corrections budget goes to treatment, and when state finances are tight, those programs are often the first thing to be cut. Even in prisons that do spend money on treatment, the philosophy on substance abuse is generally punitive rather than therapeutic. "The criminal justice system is not very forgiving," said Tombs. Where treatment centers view relapse as part of recovery, she said, prisons and probation authorities see it as a violation, evidence of a criminal unwilling to go straight. "You get a dirty urinalysis—you didn't follow the rules." For their part, corrections officials have been put in a difficult spot. They have been given a tall task: keep drug offenders off the street—or else. "For a probation or parole officer, it can be frustrating," said Tombs. "After all, how many chances do you give somebody?"

While the debate on incarceration usually centers on the addicts—a group that does not engender much sympathy—there are practical issues that must be addressed. A large number of imprisoned drug offenders are parents. For women, they are often the sole parent. What's to be done with the children? Ideally, a kindly grandmother or aunt comes to the rescue. But that's often not an option. So the children, having suffered already from living with a strung-out parent, are sent to foster care, or, more realistically, they are bounced from one foster home to another. "We have a whole generation of kids who are growing up with one or both parents incarcerated," said Tombs. "Their idea of 'family socialization' is coming to prison waiting rooms."

For taxpayers, foster care is already an increasing drain on state human resources budgets. That comes on top of the money spent to house and feed the inmates. At some point, the money runs out. Unable to build prisons fast enough, or dig any deeper into budget coffers, some states are trying alternatives to simply locking up drug offenders. Michigan has repealed some of its mandatory minimum drug sentences and has given judges the discretion to set lower penalties, or order treatment, for low-level offenders. Nebraska is considering options to serving time in prison, such as a combination of community service and vigorous monitoring by drug authorities. Kansas has passed a measure that mandates eighteen-month treatment for some offenders. Minnesota has approved a measure that would shave half of the sentences for inmates who complete a drug treatment program. "Some states are starting to reexamine their policies," said Tombs. "They're asking themselves: Does it make more sense to spend $35,000 a year for a prison cell, or $18,000 for drug treatment?"

Oklahoma has spent well over $100,000 to punish a short, stout man named Wendell, whose meth making landed him in a state penitentiary for much of the last decade. He's never been violent, except to his body and soul. Now forty-one, he's grown used to being viewed by prison guards as just another loser who ruined his life. But Wendell is no dummy. Back in high school, he was on the honor roll every quarter. He was also one tough cookie. He won the wrestling championship in his state four times. His good grades and his athletic prowess won him a full-ride scholarship to a major university in the Big Twelve Conference. He could also party with the best. While he was on campus, he preferred marijuana to alcohol because it was calorie free, and he needed to cut weight for the wrestling mat.

After he left school, he worked in water treatment as a superintendent. He made decent money. But it wasn't enough to support the meth habit he and his wife—now his ex-wife—acquired in their mid-twenties. The two of them made the stuff in their rural home and sold it. She's now in the pen, too. They have three children. The kids were nine, eleven, and thirteen when Wendell and their mom started cooking meth. "We never did it in front of them, and I'd like to tell myself that they didn't know," he said. "But if you're honest with yourself, you know that kids know what their parents are doing. They didn't know it was crank. But they knew something wrong was going on. People coming and going at all hours. And they saw their parents behave as addicts. They saw things no kids should ever see."

Wendell's kids went to his mother and then to foster homes. "Meth grabs hold of you and doesn't let go," he said, "until you lose everything in your life that you love." He shared a ten-by-twelve-foot cell with five other men. They spent much of their time talking to one another about better ways to make meth and to commit other crimes without getting caught after they got out. "Prison teaches criminals how to be better criminals," he said. "It teaches you to be hard, to be tough, to be mean. It's all about trying to prove you're a man. So you talk about ways to beat the system. You go in there because you're sick on drugs. And then you're spending your time with murderers, rapists. It's hard not to get caught up in the convict mentality." Wendell has known inmates who came to prison as nonviolent drug offenders and then were released to the streets and became violent. "You're surrounded by people who are negative. They're not asking you, 'So how long have you been clean? Keep up the good work.' There isn't any of that. It's angry talk. You hear an inmate leave a drug class and then say, 'So, how we gonna get some drugs into this place?'"

If self-esteem is important to recovery, he said, prison is the last place to build a sense of worth. "You spend your days around guards who treat you like a piece of crap. And when you get treated like that, you believe that's all you are. Everything's 'yes-sir, no-sir.' You're under their thumb. You're nothing. And they can write you up for anything, anything at all. Some guy doesn't like the way you part your hair, he writes you up. You get strip-searched. You get degraded. Day after day. They tell you when to eat, when to dress, when to go to the bathroom. They control everything about you. It's like you don't exist as a person. You know the kind of anger and resentment that builds? I mean, you put almost anybody through that kind of experience, and it's going to be pretty hard for them to get better, to think in ways that are healthy."

Being in prison means ties with loved ones are often severed, or at least badly damaged, which only makes it more difficult to find the motivation to become healthy. "Every once in a while, you see your kids on a weekend. And you've got some guard standing over your shoulder. You can't say the things that need to be said. You've got a kid asking, 'Daddy, why did you do this? Why did you end up here?' These are things that need to be addressed. But it doesn't work in that atmosphere. You can't work on relationships in the way you need to."

Nearly four years ago, Wendell started attending meetings of Alcoholics Anonymous, and he found a sponsor who helped change his way of thinking. "I came to realize that it's got to be something deep inside that changes. You've got to get determined to get better. In prison, the whole focus is on how to get out of prison. That's important to me. But the most important thing in my life has got to be my sobriety." Three months ago, he was released to a halfway house. In that environment, with counselors who seemed to care about him as a person, and surrounded by other people working hard to recover, he has found salvation. "A month ago, I got to go to my son's high school graduation," he said, his voice choking with emotion. "It was the proudest thing I've ever been able to do." He has another three months to go in the halfway house. "I've learned more about myself at the halfway house, dug more into the deeper issues, than I ever did in prison. In the pen, it was all surface stuff. Now I've got a job I go to during the day. I see real people who deal with problems, and I learn from that."

Wendell yearns for the day he makes a fresh start. He vows

to stay clean, work hard, make amends. "I'm dead-set against meth," he said. "Those days are behind me." He will need to muster all the positive attitude he can. People who go from prison to the outside world face an uphill climb, said K. C. Moon, a sentencing expert in Oklahoma. "The odds are stacked against them," he said. "There are probably fifty different kinds of jobs that are closed to an ex-con. Usually it's just the kind of entry-level, unskilled work they'd be able to do. And a lot of these guys come out of the pen in terrible debt. Maybe his child support payments were $200 a month. Now he owes $10,000. And in Oklahoma, you've got to pay back court costs, too. Where do you suppose a guy's going to get that kind of money? And we wonder why they go back to selling drugs. Maybe not. Miracles do happen. And that's what we hope for."

In Idaho, a new program gives some drug offenders a chance to go through its version of a treatment program—a prison-run boot camp—before the final sentencing by a judge. Larry, a native of Washington State, was sent to the diversionary program after being arrested on meth and credit card theft charges. His day is structured from a meeting at 5:30 A.M. until lights go out at 9:30 P.M. Each day, he must shave his head clean. It's part of the disciplinary ethos in the program that warden Theresa Baldridge describes as "a stern approach" to treatment. The program does not draw from the "medical model" of addiction common in most treatment facilities. Though most experts believe that heredity plays a role in alcoholism and drug addiction, Baldridge says the program eschews that thinking "because some offenders use genetics as a reason not to stop using." The Idaho program runs a tight ship. Infractions come with penalties, she said, including being forced to spend a class period "sitting on your hands." The inmates spend eighteen hours a week in group therapy and are required to do twenty hours of homework. Baldridge said some of the assigned workbooks focus on "thinking errors." "It's learning to change thought distortion," she said. "The kind of thinking that says, 'I didn't really steal from anybody because it came from a big corporation and they have insurance anyway.'"

It's not easy, but Larry said he's been in worse places. He was homeless for a long stretch. "I slept in the dryer at a Laundromat. I slept in Dumpsters, bus terminals. Sometimes I just walked all night." Larry is twenty-five, but acknowledges he looks much older, the consequence of meth. "I've got my teeth now, but it won't be long before they're gone. I can't brush my teeth without spitting blood." Addicts and prison officials call it "meth mouth," a common ailment among methamphetamine addicts. The corrosive nature of the chemicals used to make meth, as well as the constant grinding by wired addicts, causes severe gum disease that causes teeth to fall out. Larry also suffers memory loss. "I sometimes have trouble remembering things that happened five minutes ago," he said.

For the last several years, Larry said, his father watched in horror as he was slowly killing himself. "My dad called me in tears," he said. "It was the first time I'd ever heard my dad cry. He was begging me to stop using meth. He said no man should have to bury his son." It was a fate that would befall Larry himself. A former girlfriend—and the mother of their son—left Larry for another addict who was a member of their meth-abusing circle. When the boy was two years old, the boyfriend went into a rage and crushed the child's skull.

Baldridge said 60 to 70 percent of the people in the drug diversion program are meth addicts. They complete a six-month program, and then corrections officials issue a report to the judge. The final sentence takes into account what progress has been made in treatment. "The difference between meth and other drugs is that it takes you so quickly," she said. "It takes people who wouldn't otherwise be violent and leads them to violence."

While some judges simply lock away meth addicts or send them to boot camps, one Illinois court has tried a novel method: a form of humiliation meant to act as a deterrent to others. A prosecutor cut a deal with a woman named Penny who was charged with making meth. She could avoid jail if she allowed a photo of her devastated face to be used in a campaign against meth. There was a "before meth" and "after meth" photo. In the first photo, Penny was an attractive woman with stylish auburn hair, big expressive eyes, and a nice smile. In the second photo— taken after at least four years of meth use—she looks hideous. She is so pale she is ghostlike, looking decades older than her age of forty, with sores around her lips, her mouth hanging open to reveal cracked, rotting teeth, and eyes that stare out to nowhere. It is impossible to look at the photo and not recoil. Antidrug campaigners plastered the photo on posters and billboards in her small town, making her the object of cruel humor and derision. Before long, the photo was circulating around the nation, and even to other countries. "I am the butt of jokes on radio, and even when I go to my probation office—where my picture is on the wall—people snicker," Penny told a newspaper reporter. "I thought people would want to employ me because I've acknowledged my past and I've changed, but it's totally the opposite. I don't go out much anymore because people whisper about me and point fingers." Her life has been painful from the start. She started drinking when she was eleven. At twelve, she ran away from a troubled home. She was pregnant at thirteen and gave birth at fourteen. When she was sixteen, she married a man who would regularly beat her.

When Penny agreed to the plea bargain that allowed her photo to be used, her only other option was a thirty-year prison sentence. She sometimes wonders if it would have been easier to go to prison than to live with the taunting and callous jokes. Not long ago, the London police wrote to her and asked if they could use her picture, too. She wrote back: "I wanted to thank you for asking permission to use my photo as so many don't. This drug is evil. There is no other way to describe it. Not only the outer disfiguration is extreme, the effects it has on your insides are worse. Young people need to know that maybe for a minute you'll be skinny and full of energy, but the long-term effects are . . . I have no word to describe, but here is my story for young people to consider. It takes everything I have to walk a flight of stairs. My lungs are destroyed. I have no control over my bladder—I pee my pants all the time. I can't take a bowel movement without a laxative. And all this is just the beginning. I want no pity. I just want those young people and old to know what this stuff does to your insides as well as the outward appearance." She shudders at the notion that the ghastly picture of her—posted all over her hometown—has brought pain and embarrassment to her grandchildren. "I have ten grandkids and I don't want them to suffer," she said. "Other kids tease them about what I've done. I didn't expect this level of humiliation."

Now forty-two, Penny tries to stay focused on her recovery. In her modest home, the living-room walls are decorated with framed Bible verses. She lives as a hermit. Her purpose in life, it seems, is to serve as a kind of cautionary tale, the woman who made herself so deeply haunted, the poster child for drug abuse. She hopes her miserable image might scare some kid away from meth. Or maybe it will soften somebody's heart about a friend or family member who is tormented by drug abuse. It is impossible to look at the picture and fail to see the excruciating suffering. Who knows what might have been if someone had stepped in to help Penny, a girl who ran away before she was even a teenager, looking for some way to stop the pain, leaping headlong into the deluding, caressing, seductive arms of drugs. Her photo now advertises the pathetic woman who gave away her life to drugs. But surely it says something about those who watched, as so many did, as she teetered along the cliff's edge. And when she plummeted, the world simply wagged fingers with self-righteousness, then allowed itself a satisfied laugh at her devastating fall.

The world is full of Pennys these days, people who are dying of meth addiction. Sheriff Marvel sees them every day in his spiffy, new, overcrowded county jail in Indiana. But he is not about to make a mockery of them. He wishes that many of them were in a hospital, or a treatment center, where so many of them belong, where Penny belonged, so long ago. "It sounds funny for a police officer to say, but I'm trying to get a lot of people out of jail, because they just don't belong here," he said. "Jails should be for people we're afraid of, not people we're just mad at. And we're mad at meth users. We're mad because we can't understand how they can keep doing this to themselves; even they must know that it's harming them. We're mad at them because they won't just stop." Sheriff Marvel makes it clear that some people must be locked away for the protection of society. But for most low-level offenders, the men and women who are simply feeding a deadly addiction, the mission should be to get them healthy and back into the world, rather than let them rot in a jail cell because they suffer an addiction. Because meth making is classified as such a serious offense in Indiana—grouped along with crimes like murder—the bond is typically $200,000 or more. That kind of money is as distant as Mars for people who have lost jobs and homes, people who have made a mess of both their personal and financial lives. So Sheriff Marvel assigns one of his assistants to call the court each day and plead with the judges and prosecutors to lower bond so that some inmates can be released to treatment centers. He also hired a jail physician whose specialty is addiction, since that's the expertise most needed for inmates. He has also traveled to the nation's capital to plead with politicians to dramatically increase spending for treatment of meth addicts. "I've said, 'Listen, when this stuff finally gets to D.C., we'll get some action,'" he said. "'But don't wait for that. You can come right now to the heartland and see that it's killing our communities.'"

CHAPTER NINE

A Chance to Heal

Judge Peggy Walker watched a woman stand in her Georgia courtroom, trembling and weeping, begging to be sent for treatment for meth addiction. It is the breakthrough moment. The layers of denial have finally been pierced. There is no more pretending. Now the lying, the deceiving, the excuse making—all of it has melted against the gravity of hitting rock bottom. This is supposed to be the triumph of epiphany, the first and most important step on the road to recovery. But the woman was not whisked away to a treatment center. There were no slots open. She would have to be put on a list until her turn came. So she was left to wait, to tread water, to hold her breath. Maybe it would be a week, maybe a month, maybe longer. This desperately sick woman left the courtroom and never returned. The crushing guilt and hopelessness squeezed her like a vise until the woman could stand it no more. She took her life.

"When somebody reaches out for help, you've got to act right away," said Judge Walker, infuriated with a system that plods along while people plummet. "These are people who do love their children. They really do. They have simply become helpless because of this awful drug. And their children need them. They need them to be healthy. So then we get an addicted parent who wants to do the right thing, who agrees to go get themselves clean and healthy. But then the system says, 'No, you've got to wait. Wait until another slot opens. Wait until the next hearing.' Well, I'll tell you, if you just wait until the system is ready to help someone, they might not be there for the next hearing. They might be dead. I know it. I've seen it. And it's a crying shame."

In an ideal world, nobody would ever touch a drug as lethal as meth. They would have the sense to know that a high from a snort, a pipe, or a needle is eventually going to lay them low. The reality is that people make bad choices. They are enticed by the thrilling exhilaration of the buzz and the euphoria, as well as the initial sense of self-empowerment, that a drug can deliver. They believe they will be strong enough to stop using at will, before meth chews them up and spits them out. For those who have never gone down this wayward path, the natural impulse is to feel scorn or indignation: "We told you so." But as social policy, blame and righteousness are about as useful as telling an artery-clogged heart patient that he should simply have eaten more fresh fruit and less red meat.

While some politicians and taxpayers might resent spending more money to help addicts recover, the truth is that people who continue using drugs end up costing society more in the end. A California study found that every $1 spent on substance abuse treatment nets $7 in reduced health costs, crime, and lost productivity. And yet, untold numbers of addicts are being denied prompt care and counseling. Only about one-fifth of the spending in the nation's war on drugs actually goes to helping addicts recover. The lack of adequate care is especially acute for meth users, people who have typically lost jobs and consequently lack health insurance.

Even for those still employed, addicts seeking help often find that insurance companies don't cover the cost of residential treatment, especially for the kind of extended care necessary for treating meth addiction. As a consequence, addicts are often left to rely on treatment programs sponsored by counties and states. These centers, which were short on resources even before the meth explosion, simply cannot keep pace with the increasing demand. So addicts are put on waiting lists. In the states hardest hit by meth, the typical wait for a bed in a public residential treatment facility can be weeks or even months. That is a virtual eternity for a man or woman in the throes of meth addiction. It is a gap that gives an addict plenty of time to have a change of mind about treatment and run afoul of the law, to land in a hospital emergency room, or to end up in the morgue.

Sarah, a twenty-eight-year-old meth addict in Salt Lake City, Utah, had seen friends lose everything: jobs, homes, children. She knew she wasn't far behind. The truth was in the mirror. The sunken cheeks and sores around her lips told the story. So skinny she could barely keep her jeans up, she hadn't slept in days. "I want to get better," she told herself. "I want to get my life back." She finally decided to go for treatment. When she called social services and asked for help, they told her she would need to stand in line. The average wait for a residential treatment facility in Utah is forty-three days. She didn't know if she could make it.

A friend told her about a place called the Interim Group. It was designed for addicts like her, biding time in purgatory as they wait for a slot to open in a treatment center. Interim Group is not a treatment facility. It is not even a Twelve Step program.

There is no appeal to a Higher Power. Clients are not even required to stop using. Its mission is straightforward: to help addicts survive the wait for a slot in a treatment center. "They can say, 'I used this morning,'" said Kelly Lundberg, a psychologist at the University of Utah who started the program in 2002 with a grant of $30,000—roughly the sum it costs to keep a single drug offender in prison for a year. "And we'll say, 'Okay, we're glad you're here now.'" On the wall is a message board with information about housing and jobs. Sitting around a boardroom table in a windowless office room, the clients help each other devise strategies to get through the next day. In the past year, about one thousand addicts have walked through its doors in an office building in downtown Salt Lake City, about ten blocks from the Mormon Temple. Some addicts heard about the program through word of mouth. Others have been ordered by the courts to attend. People who attend are given two bus tokens: one to get home; one to come back.

Keeping a place in line for treatment isn't easy. With a shortage of slots for treatment, some of these programs pose requirements for staying on the waiting list to ensure that only the most motivated clients are accepted. "It's no secret that some of these treatment centers cherry-pick their clients," said Lundberg. "They're looking for the people who seem to have the best chances of recovery. So these places select the most motivated people they can. They'll tell people: 'You need to call every Monday morning between 8:00 and 8:30 to tell us you're still interested.' Can you imagine having to keep track of that? That's something most healthy people wouldn't be able to do. I couldn't."

At the Interim Group meetings, which are open six nights a week, a graduate student in counseling serves as a facilitator for group discussions. The clients are allowed to say anything they want, as long as they are respectful to others. They are allowed to speak about their ambivalence in getting treatment, a taboo in some programs, and acknowledge their stumbles. "In some programs, you can get into trouble if you talk about relapses," said Lundberg. "If you say you're not sure you want to quit, it doesn't go over well. No treatment professional wants to hear that. So people shut down. Or they just don't tell the truth. In essence, we're teaching patients to lie to us. And then we get angry when they do lie."

While this is not treatment, as such, the discussions and the sense of shared purpose among the addicts serve as support, even therapy. It doesn't always go smoothly, especially for meth addicts. Angry and paranoid from the drug use, or from the symptoms of withdrawal, a client will occasionally stand up and tell everybody in the room to go to hell and then storm out the door. More often, they support one another in the quest to get better. During one meeting, a young woman confessed that she could no longer endure the battle to stay sober.

"I want to go home and use tonight," she told the group, her head hanging low.

Another client reached out to touch the woman's shoulder. "I'm going out for coffee," he said softly. "Why don't you come with me?"

Sometimes a client will accept the offer of help, and sometimes not. An addict might leave the meeting and go home to snort or smoke or shoot up with a needle. But if that person comes back to the next meeting, he or she is met with applause, hugs, congratulations, and words of appreciation: "I was hoping you'd come back. We need you."

When they finally walk through the doors of a treatment center, meth addicts are often sky-high, and sometimes drunk as well. This state of intoxication bothers caregivers not in the least. In fact, when drivers for one residential treatment center pick up clients at the airport, they do not mind stopping at a bar, if the addict wishes to slam down a few drinks to calm the nerves. All that matters is that the addict has arrived, in whatever shape, at a place where healing can begin.

Right up until treatment, meth users might have been awake for days. The insomnia, together with the torment endured for so long by their jangled central nervous systems, causes a severe case of exhaustion. So the first order of business at a residential treatment facility, after a medical workup, is to get some sleep. It is not uncommon for a meth addict to sleep for most of the first three or four days in treatment.

In most of the traditional twenty-eight-day residential treatment centers, meth addiction is treated like any other drug or alcohol dependency. "Meth is the bull-riding of drug use—it's so intense it makes people psychotic," said Jim, an addictions counselor and a former meth user himself. "But addiction is addiction. It doesn't matter if it's Coors Light or heroin. It's not about the drug. It's about the addict."

The length and severity of withdrawal from meth can vary widely. While some addicts stop using without harsh symptoms, the experience for other addicts is harrowing: a deep depression and exhaustion. They can also feel a profound anxiety and hair-trigger irritability. They also crave the drug. The use of methamphetamine, over time, has changed the brain chemistry so that dopamine, which gives feelings of pleasure, is no longer naturally produced at sufficient levels. The drug has effectively hijacked that function of the brain. When the drug is taken away, as a consequence, so is the addict's ability to experience pleasure. In the view of the addict, going back to the drug can seem like the only way to survive. As opposed to opiates, such as heroin, there is no drug or medication that can reverse the withdrawal experience. In cases where the addict is suffering dangerous delusions, physicians will sometimes prescribe anti-psychotic medications like Haldol.

The beginning of treatment usually involves an assessment of the addict's personal and substance abuse history. When did it start? How much was used? What were the triggers? What was the reason for quitting? From there, addicts spend many hours with counselors, delving into the psychological, emotional, and spiritual core. The goal is to strip away the layers of defense and denial and to get to the essence of what's inside, what's hurting. In readings, discussions, and writing assignments, addicts are challenged to critique their faulty ways of viewing themselves, the world around them, and the drug. The object is to see the excuses for substance abuse for what they really are: intellectual deceit and con artistry.

In the mind-set of an addict, drug use or drinking is simply a rational reaction to the unfairness and abuse of the world. Counselors work to help the addict see this as being self-delusional. Similarly, the addict is challenged to accept the reality that the substance abuse has had real and lasting consequences that have harmed not only the user but an entire orbit of other people: children, spouses, parents, siblings, friends, co-workers, bosses, employees, neighbors. In group therapy, addicts come to see their own patterns of deception and denial in the stories of other addicts. When the words of others ring so familiar, the substance abuser comes to realize that certain behaviors and attitudes are hallmarks of addiction. Critically, the addict also learns that he or she is not the only person to have acted so shamefully—engaged in illicit affairs, struck a child, stole money. Once these secrets are spoken, the powerful grip of shame is lessened, especially as the addict understands how the craziness of intoxication causes people to do things they would not otherwise do. It is learning the difference between being a "bad" person and one who simply behaves badly while drunk or stoned. It is an understanding that leads to self-forgiveness, a key to becoming healthy and whole.

If there is a difference in the approach to care for a meth addiction, it is in the duration. Experts believe it simply takes longer for the body and mind to adjust to life without meth. UCLA researcher Richard Rawson, who has been studying meth addiction for more than twenty years, says treatment for the users of this drug should usually extend for six months, and perhaps significantly longer. He notes that brain scans of meth users often show significant damage to neurons. It's unclear whether this damage can ever be completely repaired, though most experts are optimistic. At the very least, says Rawson, it takes many months "to give the brain a chance to heal." During this early period of sobriety, the patient usually endures a severe case of anhedonia, the inability to feel pleasure, an extreme flatness of mood. "Everything is gray," said Rawson, speaking of a bleakness that leaves the addict convinced that "if this is how it feels to be sober, I can't do it." Rawson said the cloud generally lifts after about six months. "The trick is to get from here to there," he said. For the most part, antidepressants have been ineffective. Chemists are working to develop a nonaddictive drug that might help, but nothing has shown much promise yet.

A period of residential treatment is usually the ideal solution, since patients are monitored around the clock. Addicts in outpatient programs face a strong potential for relapse, since they go home at night to many of the familiar surroundings and social networks that serve as triggers for drug use. But meth addicts typically cannot afford private residential treatment, or there is a shortage of publicly funded centers. So Rawson and other researchers developed an outpatient program designed primarily for meth addicts.

In any setting, researchers stress that treatment must begin with the understanding that a meth addict is going to be agitated and paranoid, so sitting in a crowded room will be a frightening ordeal. Patients must be assured that their hallucinations and panic will diminish over time. They also need to be reminded that the discomfort they are experiencing comes from the drug withdrawal, which can last as long as two weeks, and not from any external factors.

With meth users, one of the major obstacles to treatment is the fear that they will be unable to perform sexually without the drug. For men, the inability to achieve an erection is often seen as catastrophic. Clients must be reminded that this is a temporary condition, and that it is the long-term use of the drug, not sobriety, that will interfere with sex life.

Treatment programs create an explicit structure and set of expectations, such as setting out a plan to attend ninety meetings in ninety days. Clients are taught to schedule activities that avoid "slippery places and people," situations where they could use the drug. In organizing a schedule, the client moves away from the frenetic pace that characterized his or her former lifestyle. Talking to meth users about the science of addiction helps them come to realize they are suffering from a disease, like diabetes or high blood pressure, and that they do not need to suffer the guilt of being a bad or lazy person. It might take two years before a meth addict's brain chemistry returns to normal, so meth addicts in recovery cannot expect to feel better quickly. The focus is on staying clean "one day at a time," even if that means "fake it 'til you make it." Family members often become involved in the recovery process so they can come to understand addictive thinking and lend the best possible support to the addict in recovery. This approach helps to remind the families that the problem is addiction, not the addicted person. Most recovering people attend self-help group meetings, such as Alcoholics Anonymous or Narcotics Anonymous, fellowships that give them a chance to tell their stories and their concerns to people who understand, to work the Twelve Steps, and to learn to live in the present and forgive themselves about the past. It is crucial to find a sponsor, an addict who has walked the burning coals and who can serve as a mentor and living symbol of hope. In time, the addicts themselves become sponsors, helping newcomers to treatment, in a framework of support that has been the paradigm of substance recovery support since AA was founded seventy years ago.

Random urine checks are a vital part of the outpatient treatment program. The idea is not to "bully" or "catch" people in transgressions, but rather to reward progress. Tests that show positive for drug use are not seen as a sign of failure, but a sign that the treatment needs to be adjusted. In these cases, the clients are asked what seems to be working about the program, and what isn't.

The horror of meth is undeniable, its power to ruin lives and families beyond dispute. It is not surprising that Illinois Attorney General Lisa Madigan has described it as "perhaps the most destructive drug ever encountered. . . . It seems to destroy everything and everyone in its path."

But there is reason for hope. Jim says that aftercare studies show that treatment of meth addicts is just as successful as it is for other drugs or alcohol. The key is getting the help and understanding that relapse, as frustrating and demoralizing as it can be, must be viewed simply as part of recovery. As the survivors can attest, it can take many battles to win the war on this drug.

Tyler bears the battle scars. He knows that treatment works, but maybe not the first or even the second time. He fell into meth use during the trauma of divorce. Drinking heavily in a bar one night, a companion told him he was getting sloppy drunk and that he made a magic potion to straighten him out. He gave him a snort of something. At the time, Tyler didn't even know what it was. "A half an hour later, I was up and walking around like I wasn't even drunk," Tyler recalled. "I was like, 'Wow, what was that?'" It was meth. Within days, he was spending every penny he had on the drug. "I was looking for something to ease the pain," he said. "I thought I found it."

Once a successful real estate agent, Tyler fell so hard that he lost everything. He quit his job, let his broker's license expire, cashed out his 401(k) investment. He found himself living in the back of his Mazda, the only material possession he had left. He would go to the county jail and then to treatment, only to find his way back to the drug and the jail cell. During one stint of sobriety, he even became a pastoral leader in a Christian rescue ministry—only to turn to meth once more. He withdrew from family and friends, too ashamed to let anyone see him as the shrunken, emaciated ghost of a man that he had become. For several years, he did not even talk to his son.

"When I was using," he said, "there was nothing else in my life but the drug." He became so paranoid he could not look into the eyes of another person. He heard voices that grew so loud he could hear nothing else. His mind was so jumbled he could not hold a conversation. His body had shrunk from 180 pounds to barely 130 pounds. His arms were covered with open sores from scratching. He even smelled of meth, an odor that can only be compared to death. To be sure, Tyler knew he was dying. But he could not stop using the drug. "The worse I got, the more empty I felt, the more I thought I needed meth." It was not long before the lights of a police car were flashing in his rearview mirror. Tyler was arrested for drunk driving—his third such offense—and possession of chemicals for making meth. He was sent to a state penitentiary.

The world could have given up on Tyler, just as he had given up on himself. He had tried treatment briefly three times, only to go back to the drug. He had finally come to the end of the line. He was resigned to rot in a cell, a fate he had come to believe he truly deserved.

America's jails and prisons are filling up with people like Tyler, lost souls who were lured into endless misery by the seductive promise of meth. But in Minnesota, where Tyler was serving his time, a new law has given addicts a choice. If they complete a recovery program, their sentences are cut in half or more. Tyler seized on this chance as if his life depended on it. And indeed it did. For eighteen months in treatment, he bared his soul to counselors, wrote about his life and addiction, studied ways to get his life back, and prayed with all his might. He wrote letters to loved ones and asked for forgiveness. "I can't take back the things I've done and all the years I've been gone," he wrote to his son. "I can only hope that you forgive me, and know that I love you." As he wrote those letters, Tyler was working on one of the vital Twelve Steps of recovery: reaching out and making amends to those who have been wronged.

Tyler was recently released from prison. He has been clean for more than two years. He now has a job with a real estate company. But mostly he is working on recovery. Every day, he gives thanks to the heavens for his gift of another chance. "I don't know what the next step will be, but God does, and I'm right where I need to be," he said.

After all the hellish trauma and searing heartbreak, after the pain of addiction and hard work of recovery, Tyler now knows the precious gift of redemption. When the doorbell rang, his heart pounded. He turned the doorknob and looked up to see a tall, handsome boy, now sixteen. He hugged his son, a boy who never gave up on his dad.

Even for those who have sunk so low they want nothing more than to die, it is possible to get beyond meth and savor life once more.

A Tennessean named David has made the journey back from hell. His wife had packed up their kids and was ready to go. Long before that, he had left them for his meth. All they could count on was his violent temper. David hated himself so much he could not stand to look in the mirror. So he took an assault rifle, loaded and locked, and pointed it under his chin. He pulled the trigger.

His face was shattered by the blast. But his life would once more become whole. As he lay in a trauma unit hospital bed in Nashville, he made a conversion of the heart, and soon the healing began. David has been sober for more than two years. It has not been easy. His face is held together with metal screws and plates. He has had seventeen reconstructive surgeries, with more to come. But his soul is at peace like never before. Faith has been the backbone of his recovery. "My kids were neglected," he said. "They feared me. I was violent." Today life is so much different. Now thirty-eight, David spends his days taking long walks with his wife, cuddling with his children as they watch *Scooby-Doo* and *SpongeBob SquarePants.* This weekend the family is going on a big fishing trip. These are the good times he never believed he would come to know. As his recovery grew stronger with each day, his oldest child, a girl of twelve, came to him with a smile she could barely conceal. "My prayers have been answered," she told him.

Chapter 1: The Magic of Meth

Guy, Jeffrey. Interview by author. Nashville, Tennessee. 2004.

"Kaitlyn." Phone interview by author. March 24, 2005.

National Clandestine Laboratory Database. "Total of All Meth Clandestine Laboratory Incidents, Including Labs, Dumpsites, Chem/Glass/Equipment." U.S. Drug Enforcement Administration Web site. 1999, 2004. www.usdoj.gov/dea/concern/map_lab_seizures.html.

911 transcript. Douglas County, Nebraska. January 5, 2005.

ONDCP Drug Policy Information Clearinghouse. "Methamphetamine." Fact sheet. November 2003. www.whitehousedrugpolicy.gov/publications/factsht/methamph/.

Payne, Rusty. Phone interview by author. 2004.

Rawson, Richard. Phone interview by author. January 20, 2005.

Substance Abuse and Mental Health Services Administration, Office of Applied Studies. "Treatment Episode Data Set (TEDS) Highlights—2002, National Admissions to Substance Abuse Treatment Services." DASIS Series: S-22, DHHS publication no. (SMA) 04-3986. Rockville, MD, 2004.

"Thomas." Phone interview by author. February 7, 2005.

"Tracing Couple's Fateful Last Steps." *Omaha World-Herald*, January 15, 2005. www.omaha.com/index.php?u_pg=1636&u_sid=1309944&u_rnd=6496685.

Note: Some interviews were conducted in confidentiality, and the names of some interviewees have been changed by mutual agreement. Pseudonyms are placed inside of quotation marks.

Chapter 2: "Mom and Pop" Labs: Hitting Hard in the Heartland

Berlin Snell, Marilyn. "Welcome to Meth Country." *Sierra Magazine,* January/February 2001. www.sierraclub.org/sierra/200101/ Meth.asp.

Fuller, Charlie. Phone interview by author. 2005.

John. Phone interview by author. 2005.

Martyny, John. "National Jewish Research Results: Clandestine Methamphetamine Laboratories." 2005. www.nationaljewish.org/ news/health-news/y2005/meth_research_results.aspx.

Payne, Rusty. Phone interview by author. 2004, 2005.

Rapstine, Pete. Phone interview by author. 2005.

Rick. Interview by author. Hot Springs, Arkansas, and over phone. 2004, 2005.

Undercover officer. Phone interview by author. 2005.

Wilgoren, Jody. "Death Humanizes Meth Issue." *New York Times,* February 10, 2005.

Chapter 3: "Works Just as Advertised": Women and Meth

Crary, David (Associated Press). "Children Often Victims of Meth Epidemic in the Heartland." *Seattle Times,* March 28, 2005. http://seattletimes.nwsource.com/html/health/2002222059_ meth28.html.

Dreisbach, Susan. Phone interview by author. 2005.

Hanson, Glen. Phone interview by author. 2005.

Jones, Cheryll. Phone interview by author. 2005.

"Kaitlyn." Phone interview by author. March 24, 2005.

Krodel, Kelly. Phone interview by author. 2005.

ONDCP Drug Policy Information Clearinghouse. "Methamphetamine." Fact sheet. November 2003. www.whitehousedrugpolicy .gov/publications/factsht/methamph/#treatment.

Chapter 4: Nobody's in Charge but Meth

"Anne." Phone interview by author. 2005.

Crary, David (Associated Press). "Children Often Victims of Meth Epidemic in the Heartland." *Seattle Times*, March 28, 2005. http://seattletimes.nwsource.com/html/health/2002222059_meth28.html.

Jones, Cheryll. Phone interview by author. 2005.

Judy. Phone interview by author. 2005.

Van Haaften, Marvin. Phone interview by author. 2005.

Chapter 5: The Poisoning of the Gay Community

"Alex." Phone interview by author. 2005.

Altman, Lawrence K. "Gays' Use of Viagra and Methamphetamine Is Linked to Diseases." *New York Times*, March 11, 2004.

Associated Press. "Gays Mobilize against Meth Addiction." *ABC News*, 2005. http://abcnews.go.com/Health/wireStory?id=638898&page=4.

Carlson, Dan. Phone interview by author. 2005.

"Evan." Phone interview by author. 2005.

Jacobs, Andrew. "The Beast in the Bathhouse." *New York Times*, January 12, 2004.

"Jason." Phone interview by author. 2005.

Jay. Phone interview by author. 2005.

Jefferson, David J. "Party, Play—and Pay." *Newsweek*, February 28, 2005.

Peter. Phone interview by author. 2005.

Poovey, Bill (Associated Press). "Meth's Sexual Effect Explains Addictions." *Miami Herald*, Dec. 3, 2004. www.miami.com/mld/miamiherald/living/health/10332066.htm?1c.

"Thomas." Phone interview by author. February 7, 2005.

Chapter 6: The Young Faces of Meth

Greenig, Mollie. Phone interview by author. 2005.

Hanson, Judy. Phone interview by author. 2005.

"Jenn." Phone interview by author. 2005.

Julie. Phone interview by author. 2005.

Life or Meth: What's the Cost? VHS. Kansas Meth Prevention Project.

Luna, Kay. "Younger Teens Are Turning to Meth." *Quad-City Times,* January 13, 2004. www.qctimes.net/articles/2004/06/12/local/export71199.txt.

Chapter 7: The Battle against Meth

Federal drug investigator. Phone interview by author. 2005.

Moon, K. C. Phone interview by author. 2005.

National Association of Chain Drug Stores. "NACDS' Analysis of Oklahoma's Touted 'Solution' to the Methamphetamine Problem." November 2004. www.nacds.org/wmspage.cfm?parm1=3421.

Pellow, Nancy. Phone interview by author. 2005.

Shaw, Gaylord. "When Meth Hits Home." *Newsday,* March 15, 2004.

Undercover narcotics officer. Interview by author. 2005.

U.S. Drug Enforcement Administration. "Kentucky." DEA Briefs and Background, Drugs and Drug Abuse, State Factsheet. 2005. www.usdoj.gov/dea/pubs/states/kentucky.html.

Woodward, Mark. Phone interview by author. 2005.

Chapter 8: Bursting at the Seams: Drug Users behind Bars

Baldridge, Theresa. Phone interview by author. 2005.

"Larry." Phone interview by author. 2005.

Marvel, Jon. Phone interview by author. 2005.

Midwinter, Janet. "Face of Meth: Former Abuser Warns Others."
Chicago Sun-Times, November 9, 2004, p. 6.

Moon, K. C. Phone interview by author. 2005.

Tombs, Barbara. Phone interview by author. 2005.

"Wendell." Phone interview by author. 2005.

Chapter 9: A Chance to Heal

"David's Story." David Parnell: Facing the Dragon—One Man's Battle
against Methamphetamine Web site. www.facingthedragon.org/
runscript.cfm?page=davids-story.cfm.

Jim. Phone interview by author. 2005.

Lundberg, Kelly. Phone interview by author. 2005.

Parnell, David. Phone interview by author. 2005.

Rawson, Richard. Phone interview by author. 2005.

"Sarah." Phone interview by author. 2005.

"Tyler." Phone interview by author. 2005.

Walker, Peggy. Phone interview by author. 2005.

Dirk Johnson is the Chicago Bureau Chief for *Newsweek* and a senior writer for the magazine. Before joining *Newsweek* in 2001, Johnson was a national correspondent at the *New York Times* for sixteen years. He is the author of *Biting the Dust.* He lives in Sycamore, Illinois.

Hazelden Publishing and Educational Services is a division of the Hazelden Foundation, a not-for-profit organization. Since 1949, Hazelden has been a leader in promoting the dignity and treatment of people afflicted with the disease of chemical dependency.

The mission of the foundation is to improve the quality of life for individuals, families, and communities by providing a national continuum of information, education, and recovery services that are widely accessible; to advance the field through research and training; and to improve our quality and effectiveness through continuous improvement and innovation.

Stemming from that, the mission of this division is to provide quality information and support to people wherever they may be in their personal journey—from education and early intervention, through treatment and recovery, to personal and spiritual growth.

Although our treatment programs do not necessarily use everything Hazelden publishes, our bibliotherapeutic materials support our mission and the Twelve Step philosophy upon which it is based. We encourage your comments and feedback.

The headquarters of the Hazelden Foundation are in Center City, Minnesota. Additional treatment facilities are located in Chicago, Illinois; Newberg, Oregon; New York, New York; Plymouth, Minnesota; and St. Paul, Minnesota. At these sites, we provide a continuum of care for men and women of all ages. Our Plymouth facility is designed specifically for youth and families.

For more information on Hazelden, please call **1-800-257-7800**. Or you may access our World Wide Web site on the Internet at **www.hazelden.org**.